THE
MAVERICK
SELLING METHOD

THE MAVERICK SELLING METHOD

Simplifying The Complex Sale

BRIAN BURNS

Library of Congress Control Number: 2009900401
ISBN: Hardcover   978-1-4415-0351-0
                   Softcover   978-1-4415-0350-3

To order additional copies of this book, contact:
Xlibris Corporation
1-888-795-4274
www.Xlibris.com
Orders@Xlibris.com
57777

Contents

Introduction

I have a small confession to make . . . I never set out to be a salesman. I actually began my career as an engineer, in part, because I assumed—naively, as it turns out—that engineers were among the best-paid employees in the company. After all, we were the ones designing and creating the products that the company marketed and sold.

My first engineering job actually had a connection to sales. Part of my duties included supporting the sales team by helping them answer customer questions and by putting together presentations that would assist clients in understanding our products. One evening though, while having dinner with some of our sales staff, I discovered something that surprised me so much that it ended up changing the course of my career and life. That evening, I found out that salespeople were among the highest paid employees in the company. In fact, they were paid substantially *more* than engineers. The reason for this discrepancy in earnings could be summed up in one word: *commissions*. As an engineer, my immediate salary remained the same, week to week, regardless of how well or poorly I performed during that period. But the salespeople in my company determined for themselves how much money they could make because their weekly paycheck was based on how successful they were at selling the company's products.

Until that evening, I had never really thought about what it might mean to have that much control over one's financial destiny. The idea that I could be in the driver's seat of my own career was extremely liberating and exciting to me. Within days of that dinner, I decided to change jobs and become a salesman.

But as you probably suspect, this shift in professions did not come without a fair amount of stress. I didn't suddenly wake up the next morning as a stellar salesman. I had many misgivings. Not only did I doubt my own propensity for the job, but I also wondered if I wanted to be associated with salespeople in general. I was not exactly what anyone would call a *natural* salesperson. To begin with, I wasn't very outgoing. Truth be told, I had been voted the shyest student in my high school. In addition, many of the sales professionals I'd known had been loud, superficial self-promoters, making me seriously question whether I wanted to join their ranks. Still, I had the drive and determination to forge ahead and the optimism to think that I could succeed without turning into someone I despised.

Like a lot of novices, I began by reading as many sales books as I could find. I studied day and night, but I never really felt that I was learning what I needed to know. After a while, I realized that these books were helpful, but they could only take me so far. So I shifted my focus and began trying to learn from salespeople themselves. I chose the best people I had worked with and spent countless hours observing them and interviewing them about all aspects of the sales process. What I discovered was that all of them shared one overriding quality that separated them from the rest of the sales force: they all were fiercely independent thinkers, who worked their own way, regardless of the expectations of their managers. In short, they were *Mavericks*—and all of them were tremendously successful, with an uncanny ability to understand what potential customers wanted and to match that knowledge with the product they were selling. While other salespeople used tricks to sneak or pressure their way into closing deals, these Mavericks were building lasting relationships with their customers. And while others in the sales staff routinely lost clients who eventually figured out what was going on, these uniquely independent thinkers were treated like valued and trusted members of their customers' teams, invited to nonsales meetings and even to company events.

The more I learned about these special people and the way they worked, the more determined I became to transform myself into one of them—and that's exactly what I have done. I have spent the last twenty years learning, practicing, improving, and teaching what I call the Maverick method. During this time, I have developed an incredible passion for the sales profession and a deep appreciation for the value that great sales professionals can bring to their clients. I also feel strongly—more strongly than ever—that the Maverick method is the simplest and most straightforward way to sell the right product to the right customer.

So what separates Mavericks from the rest of the pack? If you ask Maverick salespeople how they do what they do, their answers, at least at first, are likely to be unhelpful. "I don't know," a Maverick will say, "I just give the customers what they want." If you press Mavericks for specifics—say a technique or their preferred strategy—the answer is likely to be something vague, such as "I do whatever works."

With answers like that, it is tempting to believe that superstar sellers are endowed with some sort of "closing" gene that the rest of us did not inherit. After spending years deconstructing what Mavericks actually do, let me assure you that genetics has nothing to do with it. Instead, Mavericks succeed by proactively deploying their knowledge, skills, and intelligence. More specifically, they drive and manage the customer's decision-making process by exploiting a keen understanding of organizational dynamics, by working outside traditional selling scripts and strategies, and by using their unique talents to build long-term relationships and extract exceptional results. Mavericks are able to accomplish these objectives by continuously anticipating customer needs, by communicating value, and by tenaciously focusing on the win.

At this point, you are probably saying, "That sounds great, but how do I reach that level?" This book will show you how, and it will do so without teaching you some new sales gimmick or technique. Indeed, it would be distinctly "un-Maverick-like" to attempt to force fit you into a specific sales template or urge you to use a selling method that is not your own. Instead, this book will show you how to take the skills, knowledge, and talents that you already have and maximize them to reach your highest potential as a sales professional.

To accomplish this, I focus on a number of key areas, including,

- the natural laws of sales.
- how to develop and enhance your skills so as to separate yourself from the merely competent B-level sellers.
- how to better understand an organization's decision-making process and what you can do at each point in that process to move the deal forward,
- how to lock out your competitors or reverse decisions that favor your competitors,
- how to maximize the initial purchase, and
- how to be viewed as a team member and not simply another "vendor."

Understanding these and other parts of the Maverick method will dramatically help you attract new customers as well as build better relationships with the ones you already have. If I sound confident, it's because I am confident. I have spent years field-testing the Maverick method with real clients, and I know that it works. And more importantly, I know it can work for you.

Chapter 1

THE MAVERICK VS. THE
STEREOTYPICAL SALESMAN

Individualist carves out his or her own destiny according to nobody else's rules. In sports, we might think of a Tiger Woods or a Lance Armstrong. In business, Apple creator Steve Jobs and the word "Maverick" conjures up an image of the free-spirited cowboy—an unconventional media mogul Oprah Winfrey come to mind. And in the arts, there are countless examples—imaginative freewheelers such as Bono, Annie Leibovitz, and David Sedaris. These people seem like Mavericks to us because they have an abiding confidence in their own gifts, are driven to win, march to their own drumbeats, and often buck incredible odds to achieve their dreams.

Sales Mavericks are stamped from the same unconventional mold. While competent sellers regularly make their numbers, Mavericks far exceed their numbers. They routinely redefine what it means to be a winner, and they do it with foresight, intelligence, and élan.

Mavericks believe in limitless possibilities. They drive and manage the decision-making process by exploiting a keen understanding of organizational dynamics, by working outside traditional selling scripts and strategies, and by using their unique talents to build long-term relationships and extract exceptional results.

In this chapter, we will describe and define the Maverick seller. First, we'll differentiate Mavericks by comparing them to the rest of the sales team. Then we will show some of the common myths associated with the selling profession and how the Maverick rises above them.

The ABCs of Professional Sellers

Not all salespeople are equally skilled. For those who fare the worst in professional sales, it often comes down to a lack of motivation. The worst salespeople look at their sales jobs as temporary gigs until something better comes along. They rarely make their numbers, and except for complaining that they did not get a good territory or "there's no money in sales," they don't much care. They believe that they are meant for bigger things. We'll call those salespeople the C Players.

Then there are steady performers who range from those who have had an epiphany that led them to claw their way from C to B, to promising newcomers who are trying their best, to experienced, conscientious salespeople who make their numbers. These are the B Players.

The best of the B Players are ambitious, hard workers. But in spite of consistently reaching their sales goals, they never quite hit the ball out of the park. Not that there's anything wrong with being a dependable team member. But here's a little secret: this can be the toughest position from which to manage a successful sales career. The reason: *overcrowding*.

The vast majority of sellers fall somewhere in the B Player category, and that means the competition is stiff. The sheer number of players vying for the same slice of the comfortable compensation pie means that there are a lot of people going after the same customers using the same tired techniques and the same excuses when they don't make the sale. B Players are often their own worst enemies. They have bought into the idea that when they don't close, it is because of something outside of their control. They assume that they are doing everything right, but bad luck, timing, or fate is keeping them from the very top of their game. They keep on doing their best, but they are stuck in the status quo.

Enter the A Players—Mavericks in the Making

If you are a golf fan, you will probably remember Tiger Woods's slump during the 1997 and 1998 seasons. He didn't lose every time, but often enough that it seemed that he might not be the "phenom" the sports world thought he was. Some defectors implied that his earlier successes may have been a long string of flukes. For his part, Woods did not appear overly concerned and reported that he was working with his coach to radically overhaul his swing. When he returned to the PGA Tour for the 1999 season, he was playing better than ever before. *This is Maverick behavior.*

A Players believe that they *must* win, and just when you think they've hit a brick wall or reached the zenith of their careers, they get better. In the sales world, A Players know that they can always learn more about how to sell, and they take every opportunity to improve their game. Top sellers thrive on competition, and though they are emotionally attached to winning, they are not reckless. They win by outselling the competition—not by trickery or deception, but through meticulousness and imagination. The toughest part of selling at the highest level is simply *getting there.*

Once you've separated yourself from the pack as an A Player, you'll find that there are far fewer competitors at that level, thus clearing the way for you to be a sales superstar. But before you can become a Maverick, you have to rise above some of the myths and stereotypes about selling that have plagued this profession for too long. Indeed, despite increasing demand for professional salespeople and a growing recognition of sales as a legitimate profession, companies still don't have benchmarks for hiring professionals who excel at complex sales. Instead, they rely on stereotypes about what makes a successful salesperson, and they hire accordingly. Stereotyping is often the factor that prevents B Players from becoming As and ultimately reaching their full potential as Maverick sellers.

Going Beyond the Myths

Popular culture, urban legends, and, unfortunately, buyers' bad experiences have made unflattering stereotypes about professional sellers practically indelible, even among salespeople. While there are enough myths about professional sales and salespeople to fill a book, we've found that many of the most common myths fall into one of five categories: the "Born Salesman," the "Superstar Sales Personality," the "Single Big Sale," the "Ends Justify the Means" Winner, and the "Silver Bullet Sales Strategy."

The Myth of the "Born Salesman"

One widely held myth about successful salespeople is that they are born with an innate ability to sell anything to anyone. People assume that these aggressive, extroverted, "type A" individuals simply came into the world that way and that these traits are desirable ones to have if you are in the selling business. But a type A personality does not necessarily guarantee that someone will become an A Player in sales. In fact, one might argue that the overly aggressive, fast-talking personality is actually a *hindrance* to winning and keeping complex sales accounts because these transactions are too delicate, too nuanced, and too important to hinge upon personality. And because they involve building ongoing relationships, they are about trust rather than some kind of successful power maneuver.

It may be hard to believe, but selling, unlike eye color or left-handedness, is not an inherited trait. *Most Mavericks got to where they are not because they are naturally great salespeople, but because they are good students and good observers.* Maverick sellers earn their stripes through hard work, intellectual curiosity, experience, and a willingness to step outside of their comfort zones to go after what they want.

This myth cuts across a lot of professions. Take cooking, for example. Many of us can prepare a meal well enough to nourish ourselves and our families, and a few of us may even have a special recipe that is a guaranteed crowd-pleaser. But the same recipe in the hands of a five-star chef is usually not just better than ours or more delicious; it is sublime. Even if the home cook buys the freshest of ingredients, follows the recipe to the letter, and uses the chef's own line of branded cookware, he or she will usually not be able to replicate the professional chef's results.

Many of us can prepare a meal well enough to nourish ourselves and our families. A few of us may be regarded as good cooks by friends and acquaintances who look forward to our dinner parties. Good cooks usually have a house specialty—a recipe that they know will be a hit no matter who comes to dinner. Good cooks have mastered the recipe and may even have developed a trick or two that makes it even better.

The same recipe in the hands of a five-star chef is not merely delicious; it is sublime. Even if the home cook buys the freshest of ingredients, follows the recipe to the letter, and uses the chef's own line of branded cookware, he or she will usually not be able to replicate the professional chef's results.

This is because the chef-prepared meal is much more than the sum of its parts. Beyond the science involved in blending ingredients and applying heat, the chef's meal has risen to the level of art. Unlike the home cook, the professional chef has probably made this dish in a myriad of settings and for a variety of guests. The professional chef may have experimented with different methods, different ingredients, different complementary dishes, and produced this particular meal under a variety of conditions. His or her experience, awareness of audience, and singular style have all informed the final product.

The same is true of the Maverick seller who has elevated his or her technique to such an art form that it cannot be replicated simply by following a script. The Maverick might close a multimillion-dollar sale in sixty days. In the same situation, an average salesperson, following the same "script" as the Maverick, would struggle to get the first meeting with a qualified prospect. Salespeople doomed to remain average will blame the Maverick's success on luck, a better territory, better leads, or some other external factor.

The Myth of the "Superstar Sales Personality"

Akin to the belief that selling is simply a "gift from the gods" is the notion that all it takes to be a great seller is a great personality. If you ask your friends, associates, and maybe even your boss to describe what it takes to be a Maverick seller, their answers would lead you to believe that winning a client or closing a sale requires little more than turning on the charm. Their answers would likely include adjectives such as *gregarious, fast-talking, aggressive, charming, good-looking, charismatic, outgoing*.

If you are somewhat reserved, more comfortable in one-on-one situations than in groups, and better at listening than talking, the aforementioned expectations might sound like good reasons to pursue another line of work! If, on the other hand, you have all these characteristics and are still among the ranks of B Players, then you might assume that it's just a matter of time before you claim your rightful place among the A Players. You would be wrong either way.

Despite the stereotype, Maverick sellers' personalities are as varied as those of other professionals. *While it is important to connect with customers, Mavericks realize that the connection has to go much deeper than an appealing first impression.* Mavericks approach prospects armed with information about how the prospects' companies work and a plan not just for getting the first meeting, but also for developing relationships that lead to future sales. They leverage their unique qualities within each unique context.

Beyond a reasonable level of assertiveness, Mavericks need to be methodical and thoughtful as they pursue prospects. They need to gather information about potential customers, analyze that information, and then use it to develop a customer-centric sales strategy. Most fast-talking, hyperaggressive sellers will not even hear their customers' actual needs and, as a result, will not be able to meet customer expectations even if they win the sale.

The Myth of the "Single Big Sale"

Salespeople often fail because they don't understand that complex selling is a *process*. This flaw in their thinking makes it impossible for them to leverage the advantages that are inherent in complex sales.

Unlike consumer sales, complex sales offers professionals something that their retail brethren lack: time to strategize and plan. Even with large budgets devoted to advertising and marketing consumer products, retailers are largely dependent on customers finding *them*. Unlike complex business sellers, consumer salespeople have significantly limited time to determine customers' needs and then offer a solution.

Mavericks can take advantage of this longer sales cycle. Before meeting with a prospect, the Maverick has already developed a profile of the customer and determined that the product or service that he or she is selling meets prospective buyers' needs, fits into their budget, and complements their long-term strategic plans.

Salespeople who do not recognize that complex selling is a process also fail to recognize their role in leading customers to a close. Complex selling involves communication across multiple levels of the organizations. The people in the buying organization are usually unfamiliar with how their companies make large-scale purchases. Few companies have a clearly defined process, and so every buying experience strikes the players involved as new terrain. Mavericks not only sell their products, but they also teach their customers how to buy them. Maverick sellers find out who the key players are, what they need, and the best way to shepherd them to the goal.

Think of the last time you enjoyed a really good stay at a hotel. The tone of your stay was set from the moment you walked through the front door. Good hotels anticipate customer needs because they know a positive experience means you will come back and will pass on the information to friends and associates. So when you arrive, someone greets you at the door, takes your bags, and leads you to the registration desk. Once you've gotten your room key, you don't spend a moment wondering how you get to your room. The bellhop has already collected your bags and is guiding you to the elevator. Once you've arrived at your room, the good hotel employee will have already anticipated your questions, letting you know where the fitness center is located, how to access the Internet connection, how to adjust the room temperature, where to find a good local restaurant, etc. From clean towels to subway train schedules, no detail is too small.

Mavericks do this for their customers as well. They set the tone so that the labyrinthine process of corporate buying becomes a relatively painless process. Salespeople fail when they do not recognize that their job is to anticipate and *direct* the sales process. Left up to the customer, the process gets weighed down with miscommunication, overlooked connections, and forgotten steps, all leading to a failed sale.

Unlike consumer sales, complex corporate sales involve a great deal of time spent in front of customers. In complex sales, the customer is not a single person. Rather, multiple people at different levels of the organization are involved in making the decision to buy. The buying process can take anywhere from several weeks to several months.

Mavericks know that establishing rapport with different people in the organization is critical to closing the deal. He or she also knows that developing rapport across the organizational chart requires a keen understanding of the customer's business and close listening to how people in the organization describe their own interests. *Mavericks understand that the sale is not about the seller. Complex sales is about listening and responding to customers' business needs.*

The Myth of the "Ends Justify the Means" Winner

Popular culture has not been kind to the image of the professional salesperson. When they aren't depicted as washed-up Willy Lomans, they are shown to be pathologically unscrupulous manipulators who will go to any extreme to make the sale or close the deal.

In the film adaptation of David Mamet's *Glengarry Glen Ross,* Alec Baldwin plays a ruthless manager (Blake) who "motivates" his sales team with a barrage of verbal abuse culminating in a promise to fire all but the two top performers after one week. With images like that, it's no wonder that "professional sales" has a vaguely oxymoronic ring to it.

Although it is an extreme portrayal, the character of Blake is an interesting reflection of corporations' own myths about sales. In many companies, there is a prevailing notion that anyone with an aggressive personality and bills to pay has the makings of a successful salesperson, and that idea gives credence to another more unfortunate assumption: that salespeople are a dime a dozen. They are easily replaceable.

We have all heard stories about salespeople who will go to any lengths to make a sale from exaggerating their products' capabilities to outright lies. Even professional salespeople have been on the wrong end of a transaction with the unctuous used car salesman who never provides a direct answer, pressures you into buying things you don't need, and shoves a contract under your nose with a lot of hidden fees. There are stories about salespeople for whom "getting one over" on a customer is practically a kind of sport. There are even stories about salespeople who have duped entire communities into buying products and services that didn't even exist or that they didn't need. At worst, salespeople have sold products that were dangerous, or even fatal.

The good news is that most salespeople are not devious misanthropes who would just as soon sell cancer as a cure. However, the sales profession has only recently begun to establish organizations whose missions include codifying ethical practices and standards for their members. Membership in such organizations is voluntary, but as sales managers begin to seek out benchmarks for qualifying good additions to their sales teams, the organizations will become more influential in setting professional standards. The bad news is that bad news travels fast and far.

When customers have a bad sales experience, they tell everyone. People share their nightmare story, it gets embellished along the way, and pretty soon it has become a more pervasive perception that is difficult, if not impossible, to shake. When these bad perceptions take root, they tarnish the reputations of even the most honest salespeople.

Mavericks' understanding of the importance of observing solid professional ethics goes deeper. Top sellers do not see sales as single occurrences to be forgotten about as soon as the ink dries on the sales contract or purchase order. *Mavericks recognize that every contact with a customer is an opportunity to make the next sale.* Therefore, keeping customers' best interests in mind is in the seller's best interest as well.

The Myth of the "Silver Bullet Sales Strategy"

B Players can spend their entire careers searching for a sales strategy that will make them into superstars. They take every course and read every book. At the end of every seminar or conference, they are excited by the possibilities, and then when the demands of work kick in, they put aside their newfound sales wisdom and go back to selling the way that they did before. They continue to make their numbers, but they do not rise above B level into the elite ranks of the Maverick.

This myth comes from *inside* rather than outside the sales profession. Sales managers who dutifully ensure that their teams get the latest and greatest in sales training perpetuate the idea of the silver bullet approach. Sales training is fine but, in and of itself, rarely begets Mavericks.

The reason is, with a few exceptions, Mavericks are mostly eclectic about sales techniques and strategies. Mavericks use what they've learned and draw on their past experiences to develop a customer-centered sales strategy. In particular, Mavericks know that the best way to make a sale—and future sales to the same customer—is by learning everything that they can about prospective customers, having a deep understanding of their own products, including how that product stands up in the marketplace and how it measures up to their competitors' offerings.

Not only do Mavericks determine which strategies to employ on a customer-by-customer basis, they will also use different approaches with different people within a single company. For instance, the Maverick may stress his product's ease of use with the firm's chief technology officer while talking more about price and value with the chief financial officer.

Mavericks know that there is no magic script for selling all products to all customers. They know that their customers do not follow the same buying scripts. If they did, the buying process would be easier, and professional sales would not be as lucrative as it is for the best salespeople. In addition, few companies have explicit mechanisms for buying high-dollar products, and fewer still have a single job function that is devoted to buying those products. Upon the first sales call, apart from learning the customer's needs, the Maverick's first job is to learn the company's buying process and then lead the buyers through it.

The beauty of Maverick selling is that it can be learned. So even if you were born with some of the personality traits that are frequently stereotyped as "sales personalities," you can take comfort knowing that you are not bound by your heredity. You can learn how Mavericks achieve their levels of success and, by modeling their behavior, become a Maverick too.

In the next chapter, we will get inside of the mind of the Maverick and look at some of the qualities that distinguish him or her from the pack.

The ABCs of Professional Sellers

A-Level Salespeople

- Smart, intensely competitive, and highly self-motivated to be the best.
- Ethical and seek to balance being fair and being right.
- Confident that they can perform at a higher level than most.
- Leaders who rise above the noise and take responsibility for making things happen.
- Creative and regularly close sales that others thought impossible.
- Valuable advisors and partners in their customers' businesses.
- Drivers in the sales process who lead their customers to closing.
- Emotionally attached to winning.
- Savvy about the competition and their sales strategies.
- Visionary about their success in every sales situation.
- Aware of what they don't know.
- Proactive and anticipate and manage problems and detours during the sales process.

B-Level Salespeople

- Consistent performers who regularly achieve 80% to 100% of their numbers.
- Capable sellers who never quite knock it out of the park.
- Often reactive, and this keeps them from becoming Mavericks.
- Often their own worst enemies because they believe that they know everything about sales and that they are already doing everything possible.
- Usually not drivers in the sales process. They tend to wait to be directed by their customers.
- Often distracted from sales duties by busy work.
- Frequently detailed and structured, but miss the forest for the trees.

C-Level Salespeople

- Poor performers who rarely make their numbers.
- Not as sales savvy as B Players.
- Completely reactive in sales situations, but proactive in scheduling time off.
- Biding their time until a better opportunity presents itself.
- Sometimes mistaken as B Players because they focus on the selling inside an organization.
- Retired and forgot to mention it to HR.

Chapter 2

THE MIND OF THE MAVERICK

In the first chapter of this book, we touched on some of the myths about professional sales and professional sellers. In this chapter, we are going to go inside the mind of the Maverick, to see how he or she ticks. We will look at some of the qualities that A-Level Players possess and how Mavericks take these qualities to a whole new level. We'll discuss how Mavericks think, what they know, and why companies need them.

What Makes the Maverick Different?

Mavericks go against the grain. They look at whatever they do with a new set of eyes, reinventing what it means to compete and to win. Their vision is singular, at times even perversely iconoclastic. Some would say that not only do they find new ways of winning for themselves, but they also make sure their customers win as well. Interestingly, the word "Maverick" comes from an actual person— Samuel Augustus Maverick (1803-1870)—who was a Yale graduate and signer of the Texas Declaration of Independence. A successful land speculator, Maverick refused to brand the cattle on his range. As a result, the word "Maverick" entered our lexicon to mean both an unbranded range animal as well as anyone who refuses to "run with the herd." It has become a synonym for stubborn and resourceful independence.

Mavericks thrive on competition and the adrenaline rush that comes from doing the impossible. For sales Mavericks, this means closing a sale, and the tougher the challenge, the better. They actually seek out difficult customers and more complex sales because the thrill of doing what others think of as impossible is a rush for them. Although every Maverick has his or her own approach, and this approach usually varies from customer to customer, they do have traits in common.

Later in this book, we will examine some of the skills and strategies Mavericks uses to their advantage. For now, let's take a closer look at some of the qualities Mavericks must have to succeed.

The Qualities of a Maverick

To some extent, all Mavericks share the following five characteristics:

- Proactive
- Intelligent
- Motivated
- Competitive
- Creative

Like the rest of us, Mavericks have strengths and weaknesses, and they may be more effective in some of these areas than others. Because they are resourceful and adaptable, Mavericks play to their strengths in any given situation. Likewise, some people may have a personality that contains all the characteristics in this list, but this does not necessarily mean they are Mavericks. In the hands of a Maverick, however, these qualities can mean the difference between scrambled eggs and quiche.

Proactive

Mavericks are not ones to sit and ruminate. Rather than kibitzing at the water cooler with other salespeople about the challenges of selling, Mavericks are out there connecting with prospects. A Players know that to ensure the highest ratio of closed sales to the number of prospects, they have to drive the process. Rather than asking a customer to tell them what to do next, Mavericks lead their customers through the buying process to ensure that they close the deal.

A good example of a proactive Maverick is entrepreneur Elon Musk who, before his thirty-fifth birthday, founded five cutting-edge technology companies. At age seventeen, Musk left his native South Africa for North America where he lived on as little as a dollar a day while a university student. A little more than five years later, Musk founded his first company, Zip2, a publishing software provider. After selling the firm for more than $300 million, Musk cofounded PayPal, the wildly successful online payments service, which he eventually sold to eBay in 2002 for $1.5 billion. At this point, Musk decided to begin not one, but three new businesses, each in a different, up-and-coming industry. One of his firms, SpaceX, is developing rockets to take cargo and people into orbit for much less than governments charge. Another of his new businesses, Tesla Motors, makes electric cars. His third new venture, SolarCity, is a solar panel installation company. In his relatively brief career, Musk, like many Mavericks, has shown an uncanny ability to spot new trends and to act quickly to capitalize on them.

Intelligent

Regardless of their educational background, Mavericks are smart, knowledgeable, and open to learning more. They have to be.

In order to consistently sell above their numbers, Mavericks must be "renaissance" men or women, proficient in a number of disciplines in addition to sales. Professional sellers master the intricacies of the products that they are selling, of course, but they learn a great deal about other subjects too.

Accounting and economics are useful to a Maverick who is learning about a prospective customer. Being able to read and understand a prospect's profit-and-loss statements helps the seller determine whether or not the firm is in a position to buy the product.

Understanding conditions in the prospect's industry gives the Maverick more clues about prospects' buying position, such as whether or not the industry is looking to expand its capital spending.

Organizational psychology helps one understand different companies' cultures. While "corporate culture" may sound esoteric, consider that understanding how a company is structured—and this involves much more than just the organizational hierarchy—gets salespeople past the gatekeepers and to the decision makers and purse holders that much faster. But it is also invaluable information for figuring out where the pockets of resistance are, who has the ear of management, and areas within the company that may not be working optimally.

A good example of a highly intelligent business Maverick is Meg Whitman, CEO of eBay for ten years who retired in 2008 and may be a contender for governorship of California in 2010. With a BA in economics from Princeton and an MBA from Harvard Business School, Whitman took the helm at eBay when it was a small auction Web site with just thirty employees and annual revenues of $4 million. A brilliant strategist and arguably the most successful female tech CEO ever, Whitman hired world-class executives, focused on growth, and made customer service a top priority. She also addressed many of the technical glitches that plagued the company's Web site in its early years and used her brand-building expertise to turn the company into an e-commerce powerhouse. Whitman had strong consumer instincts, and she kept customers coming back, even when they were frustrated, by soliciting their feedback and keeping them informed. Like many Mavericks, she provided strong leadership but had enough insight and intelligence to know when to defer to other people's strengths and when it was time to exit the stage and let new blood take over.

Motivated

Mavericks don't think of sales as "just a job." Sales is a passion, and whether it is the ability to have substantial control over their career—the lure of above-average earnings—or the thrill of creating markets where previously none existed, something drives Mavericks beyond a need to pay the bills. *Motivation* is the catalyst that propels B Players to the elite league of A Players. An example of this kind of driving incentive is Philippe Petit, a French high-wire artist born in 1949 who became famous for his illegal walk between the Twin Towers in New York City in the summer of 1974. For years, Petit had dreamed of walking between the world's two largest buildings, and it took a massive amount of planning (and not a little subterfuge) to make it happen. Among other things, Petit made a model of the towers based on articles he had read so he could plan for how much walking cable he would need. He also had to take into account such formidable problems as the swaying of the buildings due to the wind and the police and workmen who made access difficult.

Petit did something that no one felt was possible and what most would have believed suicidal. He did not view this feat as scary but rather as the thrill of a lifetime. The walk between the buildings, which were a one-fourth mile high, was done without any safety ropes or parachute. He did not just cross them once, he crossed them EIGHT times and enjoyed the experience so much that he sat in the middle of the wire, taunting the police at the top of each of the towers. At one point, he even lay down on the wire and chatted with a seagull overhead. Later, when asked why he did the stunt, Petit said, "When I see three oranges, I juggle. When I see two towers, I walk." (Now, that's motivated.)

Competitive

Mavericks don't just like to win. They hate to lose. They hate to lose much more than B Players do, and on the rare occasions when they don't make a close, they take total responsibility for the loss. They do not blame the buyers or their territory or the competition. They accept that they were somehow "off their game." When people talk about professional sales as a game, as in "the sales game," it rings true for Mavericks. It isn't enough for Mavericks to close a single deal. They want a win for their customers too. When customers sign on the dotted line and feel confident that their purchase was the right solution for their business at the right price and from the right seller, the customer wins, as well as the seller. Win-win? Yes. In fact, Mavericks turn it into a compounding win because in satisfying the customer, the Maverick is setting up to win the next sale from the same customer.

Pain is temporary. Quitting lasts forever.
—Lance Armstrong

Lance Armstrong, who won the Tour de France a seemingly unbeatable seven times, has a level of competitiveness and an openness to new information that makes him a true Maverick. Armstrong has said that one of the things that gives him an edge is that he can withstand more pain than anyone else, and he beats A-level cyclists like Jan Ullrich and Ivan Basso because he has redefined how to train and how to win. For example, Armstrong has developed a high lactate threshold that allows him to maintain a higher cycling cadence and in a lower gear. While his competitors often use a higher gear and brute strength in trials, Armstrong's faster cadence means he has greater muscular efficiency—his legs don't tire as quickly, and he recovers faster. Known for being an indefatigable trainer, Armstrong spent much of his training time focused on how to develop and maintain this high cadence style. One gets the sense that whether it was improving his lung capacity or discovering a better protein bar, Lance was on it. Winning to Lance is the only alternative—to him, as to every Maverick, there is no second place.

Like the Maverick athlete, Maverick sellers must be willing to change, to learn new skills and technologies, to understand that what worked with Harry may not work with Paul, to recognize what they do best, and then maximize it to great purpose.

Creative

We don't usually associate creativity with entrepreneurs or salespeople. But it is an essential skill for the Maverick. Thinking outside of the normal range or beyond the conventional and being bold enough to articulate and implement solutions based on that thinking is an everyday occurrence with Mavericks.

A good example of this skill is Guy Laliberté, one of the two founders of the world-famous *Cirque du Soleil.* Although he began modestly as an accordion player and stilt walker, Laliberté would go on to create a billion-dollar company that has redefined what the modern circus means. Laliberté, who is known for his exacting standards, his financial independence, and his willingness to take risks, created an entertainment experience that synthesized various circus styles from around the world, but also took the circus beyond the traditional "rings and circus animals" approach. He has created nearly two dozen different shows over the years and is always looking for new ideas, not only for *Cirque*, but also in other business ventures as well.

Although he has been wildly successful, it was not always that way for Laliberté. Over the years, he has had to be flexible, imaginative, and optimistic in the face of potential bankruptcy, disenchanted performers, creative differences, and more. (One year, one of the big top tents caved in because of the additional weight brought on by rainwater!) Throughout it all, Laliberté stayed true to his vision and constantly challenged himself to think outside of the boxer, tent!

A sales Maverick can sell the same product to two different customers to solve completely different, but very legitimate, business problems. They keep themselves adaptable to different people, different businesses, and different ways of approaching a problem.

What Mavericks Know

The first thing that all Mavericks know is, perhaps, the most important factor in their success in professional sales: *Mavericks know that they don't know everything.* Like Tiger Woods dismantling his trademark swing and coming back stronger than ever, Mavericks know that being open to continuous learning keeps them at the top of their game.

B Players are often trapped by the belief that there is a finite amount of information that a sales professional can acquire. But Mavericks know that in sales, as well as any endeavor, learning needs to be a lifelong habit. Learning means more than formal training. Indeed, sales training, though often helpful, does not make a Maverick. Mavericks learn from every source imaginable, from books and formal lectures to observing how a client responds to a certain sales pitch.

Like all elite sellers, *Mavericks know that it's the customer, stupid.* In other words, when a Maverick meets with a prospect, he or she knows that in most cases, the customer doesn't care about products. Customers are motivated to buy when they need and discover a solution to a business problem. Mavericks sell the vision of the end result. Sales prospects buy improved productivity, higher profits, and happier customers when they buy from a Maverick. A product just happens to come with it.

The corollary to "it's the customer, stupid," is the maxim that selling is not telling. In fact, a good deal of selling is listening. *Mavericks know that people act in their own best interests and would much rather hear themselves talk than listen to you.* If the sales professional is doing all the talking, he or she will not understand the customer's vision for the end result.

Mavericks know their competition. They keep abreast of new products, changes in management, fluctuating sales, and other conditions that affect their competitors. Having this information means that the Maverick is in the enviable position of understanding how their competitors position their products in the market, which allows them to counter competitors' sales pitches preemptively.

Lastly, rather than relying on a single sales strategy, *Mavericks know that one size doesn't fit all.* Mavericks master a number of sales techniques and customer approaches—remember, they are always learning and modeling—and then employ the strategies and tactics that best suit the selling situation. Typically, Mavericks do not subscribe to any one sales method or strategy. Instead, they use certain aspects of different strategies to ensure that they speak to their prospects' needs.

Why Companies Need Mavericks

Companies that cannot find—or create—markets for their products will go out of business. Sales is vital to corporate success. While corporations know this on a visceral level, they are not usually conscious of it. It's like knowing you should exercise and eat healthy foods but not doing anything about it until you get sick. A company that ignores the knowledge and impact of their sales force shouldn't be surprised when things begin to fall apart.

Corporations also focus their attention and resources on their most apparent attributes: their products. They hire skilled engineers to develop and deploy them. They hire professional marketers to position products in the marketplace. Finance departments secure funding for product development, and they create budgets to ensure that they meet revenue targets.

What companies rarely acknowledge, though, is what their top salespeople know best: customers often are indifferent about products. Their main concern is with business results. In the realm of complex, business-to-business sales—the kind on which this book focuses—companies are more concerned with improving their productivity and staying competitive. *The best salespeople—the ones that we are calling Mavericks—know that their job is not to sell products so much as it is to solve their customers' pressing business problems.*

Companies devote significant portions of their budgets to developing and promoting their products and services. Advertising and marketing can do a great job of making prospects aware of a company's offerings, but their efforts only go as far as showcasing the product along with a laundry list of its attributes. Economies of time and space limit their efforts, and they are simply not equipped to focus on client needs. Let's face it: a one-page print ad or a thirty-second television spot can attract attention, but those media do not speak to individual companies' specific problems.

Maverick salespeople, on the other hand, can do what no ad campaign can: they ally themselves with their customers and lead them through the sales process. When Mavericks are selling high-dollar products or innovative products at the cutting edge, they are even more valuable both to their customers and to their companies.

Mavericks Are a Company's First Line of Defense

Any decision to make a major business purchase is a decision to make a change, and as a rule, most people hate change. The complexity that is inherent in business sales rarely has anything to do with the quality, and certainly not the quantity, of available products. What makes the business sale so challenging is that the salesperson does not have to convince a single rational entity called "the corporation" to buy a product; rather, the salesperson has to calm the risk aversion of every person involved in making the purchase.

This is where Mavericks excel and where corporate sales strategies fall short. Too often, companies assume that a salesperson is a salesperson and that the Maverick is just lucky. The fact is there are several instances when companies want to ensure that they are sending their A Players out into the field. Those situations include,

- when there are no inbound leads,
- when the product is an innovation and there is no existing market,
- when product cost exceeds $100,000, and
- when the customer is a senior executive who needs a salesperson who can speak to them in business terms.

The reason companies should have their best A Players handling these transactions is that these situations add another dimension of complexity to the already challenging arena of complex business sales. Mavericks' ability to employ artful solutions, and their knowledge on how to navigate companies' buying structures, makes them critical to winning sales when any of these conditions exist.

The next chapter, "The Natural Laws of Sales," begins to walk you through what it takes to succeed in complex sales. It describes the laws by which people make decisions and explains how salespeople can leverage those laws to understand the selling terrain and outsmart their competitors.

Chapter 3

THE NATURAL LAWS OF SALES

Whenever you really want to learn and become great at a particular profession, you must first understand the guiding principles or laws of that vocation. Regardless of whether or not a person acknowledges the truth, sales, as much as any endeavor in life, has laws that explain the natural process and organization associated with the activity.

What is the first thing anyone does when he/she begins to play a new game? He or she learns the rules because without understanding the rules, there is no comprehension of how the game is played. A sale, just like a game, has rules, but unfortunately, these rules are not written on the inside of any box, and all too often, the rules to the game of sales are learned the hard way. In order to understand the Maverick selling method, a person must understand the laws that govern and rule the complexity of sales. The laws will give insight into what can be expected, will occur, and then happen next.

As there are four immutable laws (or forces) that govern the universe,[1] so there are four immutable laws (or forces) governing

---

[1]   Gravity, electromagnetism, strong nuclear force, weak nuclear force

sales. These laws do not have to be obeyed from a legal sense; rather, the laws must be obeyed in order to succeed. Like gravity. A man may leap off a tall building shrieking, "I don't believe in gravity." However, he doesn't break the law of gravity. It breaks him. For example, there is no legal requirement to obey the law of gravity, but if a person does not believe in gravity and jumps from a building, the law of gravity causes serious injury, and therefore, it triumphs. Failure to recognize these laws for what they are will result in disaster. The Maverick selling method, while not governed by the rules of sales, is in every sense attuned to the laws of sales. These laws of sales are as follows:

1. Everyone will ultimately act in his own self-interest.
2. Self-interest, properly understood, is a Good Thing.
3. People are generally risk averse for gains and risk seeking for losses.
4. What is not overtly positive is covertly negative.

These are the governing forces that shall be considered in some detail. In addition, some laws (secondary laws) are not universal (like the second law of thermodynamics) but hold true *in their realm.* These secondary laws are as follows:

- Nothing happens unless you make it happen.
- Divide and concur.
- It is not the product.
- If you know what's going to happen, then you will know what to do.
- You know how to sell, but your prospect does not know how to purchase.
- Set the rules and be prepared to change them.

Let us begin with the four laws of sales.

1. *All things being equal, everyone will ultimately act in his own self-interest.* This basic fact or law or dictate of human nature is best evidenced in game theory and, more specifically, in the non-zero-sum game known as the Prisoner's Dilemma.

The Game

Two bad guys, referred to as Bonnie and Clyde, are caught near the scene of a crime. The police interrogate them separately. Each has to choose whether to confess and implicate the other. If both confess, they will each serve ten years, half the maximum for cooperating with the prosecution. If neither confesses, they will each serve one year on a weapons charge. If one confesses, implicating the other, while the other remains silent, the first will go free, while the silent one will serve the maximum penalty of twenty years in prison.

The strategies in this case are simple: squeal or don't squeal. The payoffs (or penalties) are the prison sentences. This can be expressed simply in a typical game theory payoff table:

		Clyde	
		squeal	don't squeal
Bonnie	squeal	10, 10	0, 20
	don't squeal	20, 0	1, 1

The table reads thus: Each bad guy chooses one of the two strategies (Bonnie opts for one row in the table, Clyde decides on a column to play). If Bonnie and Clyde both sing like canaries, they each get ten years. If Bonnie rats Clyde out, and Clyde remains silent, Bonnie goes free, while Clyde serves twenty years. If Bonnie doesn't squeal and Clyde does, Bonnie goes to prison for twenty years while Clyde goes free. If neither confesses, they each serve one year (on the weapons charge).

What then are the rational strategies if both want to minimize the time they spend in prison? Bonnie might reason something like this: "Two things can happen: Clyde will either confess or he won't. If he confesses, and I don't, I get twenty years—ten years if I confess too—so in that case, it is best if I confess. On the other hand, if Clyde does not confess, and neither do I, I get a year, but in that case, if I confess, I can go free. Either way, it's best if I confess. Therefore, I will confess."

However, Clyde will likely reason in the same way—both will therefore confess and go to prison for ten years each. While if they had acted irrationally, and kept quiet, they each could have gotten off with one year a piece.

That is a lengthy narrative used to say that people, when they act rationally, do what is in their own best interest, a principle that is true for buyers as well as sellers. An extreme example of this principle manifests in the example of a sales manager who failed to recognize this law for what it is: he would call prospects toward the end of the quarter and explain that his employee bonus depended on closing that particular sale. Customers may have wondered why they should care and what is in it for them.

Mavericks understand that their jobs would be easy if they only had to sell to companies. All they would have to do is demonstrate to the company that their product is the best fit for the need. However, salespeople do not sell to nonhuman entities called companies; rather, the sales are made to individuals who want to ensure that their best interests are served even while professing to have the good of the company at heart. Mavericks also know that individuals may have interests that sometimes conflict, and it is the salesman's job to ensure that all the players feel that the needs of the individual and the company have been met when the final deal is stuck.

2. *Self-interest, properly understood, is a Good Thing.* Montaigne said long ago, "Even if I should not follow the straight road because of its straightness, I would follow it because I have found by experience that when all is said and done it is generally the happiest and most useful."[2] Tocqueville noted, "In the United States there is hardly any talk of the beauty of virtue. However, they maintain that virtue is useful and prove it every day. American moralists do not pretend that one must sacrifice

---

[2] Michael de Montaigne and Donald M. Frame, "Of Glory," in *The Complete Essays of Montaigne*, II:16, 473.

himself for his fellows because it is a fine thing to do so . . . . They therefore do not raise objections to men pursuing their interests, but they do all that they can to prove that it is in each man's interest to be good."[3] Finally, Marcus Fabius Quintilian points out that "providence has given this gift to man, that the honorable is the most profitable."

The lesson learned from all this is in fact one of the laws of sales: self-interest, properly understood, is a Good Thing. This is to say that what is good for the individual is also good for the community at large. What makes this law tricky is that it applies to salespeople as much as it does to their prospects. What sets Mavericks apart is that they understand that acting in their prospects' best interests *is* in their greatest interest.

When Mavericks approach a sale, they go in knowing that acting in the prospect's best interest means acting in the best interest of *all* the individuals involved in making the buying decision. Although each person believes that he or she is doing what is right for the company, the truth is that they are looking out for themselves first and the companies needs second.

Mavericks know this and use it as part of their sales strategy. A Players ask how each person in the process will benefit from closing the sale: *What's in it for them?* Asking this question, and being proactive about getting the answers, means that the seller will be able to present all communications in terms of how each person in the buying chain will benefit from the Maverick's solution.

For example, knowing that a key person involved in making the buying decision is up for a promotion means that you can speak to how your product or service will serve that individual's future success. In that case, you are selling two things: career advancement and esteem from the person's bosses. It doesn't end there. When the up-and-comer's bosses are involved in the sale, Mavericks also ask themselves about the outcomes the bosses hope to gain from the purchase. Will choosing your product over a competitors' equal a "win" for the manager embroiled in an

---

[3] Alexis de Toqueville, "How the Americans Combat Individualism by the Doctrine of Self-Interest Properly Understood," in *Democracy in America*, 524–525.

ongoing political rivalry? What of the rival? If that person is also involved in the buying decision, can you demonstrate that your product or service will show up in his or her "win" column as well. If someone else in the chain has another vendor at the top of his or her list, can you show that your solution will resolve the problems that keep him or her awake at night more effectively than the competitor's solution?

While learning about the company as a whole and selling to its best interest is vital to closing complex sales, learning to navigate the internal and interpersonal workings is just as important. Solid B Players make it their business to comb a prospect's Web site for information about its financials, customers, and market position. Exceptional B Players find out about the prospect's competitors. Mavericks are the A Players, and they go further.

3. ***People are generally risk averse for gains and risk seeking for losses.*** This is proven as a law over and over again in examples such as Wheel of Fortune and in countless gambling studies. The *escalation bias* also comes into play. In behavioral finance, *escalation bias* causes investors to invest more in money-losing investments. People are willing to compound losses for the sake of trying to "make it better" or prove they can "fix a wrong" all the while neglecting investment in successful ventures because there is no big win.

    When we are winning, we are risk averse; when we are losing, we are risk seeking.

    Buyers who are comfortable with the status quo are risk averse. "Building the pain" is a basic principle of consultative selling that has roots in behavioral psychology. Getting someone to buy into an innovative or disruptive technology requires precisely that he is not comfortable with the status quo. Indeed, they must feel like they are losing in order to overcome risk aversion. The Maverick intuitively understands that building the pain to a critical mass is crucial to making the sale.

4. ***What is not overtly positive is covertly negative.*** If you are not getting clear, positive feedback from a prospect, assume that something is wrong. No one likes to give or be on the receiving end of bad news. However, it is incumbent upon the salesperson to get to the bottom of any feedback that is not obviously positive, and that includes getting no feedback at all.

It is tempting to believe that a silent prospect is "just busy." It is comforting to believe that you are still being considered even when the prospect has stopped returning your calls or has started to miss commitments. In sales, deluding oneself into believing that tepid news or no news is good news is referred to as *happy ears* and that delusion leads to missed sales.

Here is the thing: we have had customers issue purchase orders for our products all the while telling our competitors that they were still weighing their options. It isn't that the prospects are mean-spirited; rather, it is that the customer does not want to be the bearer of bad news.

> *Though it be honest, it is never good*
> *To bring bad news; give to a gracious message*
> *A host of tongues, but let ill tidings tell*
> *Themselves when they be felt.*[4]

The desire to avoid the uncomfortable position of being the one to tell the salesperson, "Sorry, we went with Vendor X," hearkens to the first Maverick law: delivering bad news rarely serves the prospect's best interest.

Mavericks do not suffer from *happy ears* because they do not initiate the sale then stand in the wings waiting to be chosen. Mavericks elicit feedback from prospects throughout the buying process and enforce a cadence of communication that, if broken, signals that something is wrong. As they lead prospects from the initial sales call to signing a contract, A Players check to see how all the people involved in the buying decision are feeling. Remember: at its most basic level, deciding to buy something is emotional. If this was not the case, consumers would always forego the over-the-top SUV in favor of a fuel-efficient economy car that reliably transports them to work every day.

Such are the four immutable laws of sales. Let's look now at the secondary laws.

---

[4]   William Shakespeare, *Tragedy of Antony and Cleopatra*, Act II, Scene 5.

Nothing Happens Unless You Make It Happen

Newton's first law of motion, sometimes called the law of inertia, and is often stated thusly: An object at rest tends to stay at rest and an object in motion tends to stay in motion with the same speed and in the same direction unless acted upon by an external force.[5] Companies at rest tend to stay that way unless acted upon by an external force. Lack of change is easy and comfortable. Unless there is some catalyst that propels an organization to buy something, it will not. Companies are moved to invest in high-dollar products and services when they perceive an imminent threat or there is an obvious and justifiable opportunity.

Mavericks know this and understand that what separates them from the pack is their ability to propel a company successfully to a closed sale even when external (or, often, internal) forces conspire to slow or stop the process. Whether companies are motivated by a threat (i.e., updating their computer systems in time for the new millennium), or an opportunity (i.e., enough capacity to handle an expected surge in demand for their products online), Mavericks do not trust the company's natural workflow to end in a closed sale. Mavericks lead and control the process. Leaving a sale up to the natural flow allows outside forces—like the prospect's undefined and poorly understood internal buying procedures—to slow or stop the process, thereby providing an opportunity for a competing salesperson to take the lead and the sale.

Divide and "Concur"

This is not a typo. The expected "conquer" is not actually in the Maverick lexicon because they always seek the win-win solution. A Maverick sale is no place for conquest. However, it *is* a place for division, at least initially. The Maverick divides to gain cooperation or concurrence. He meets separately with each of the stakeholders in the client's decision chain, seeking *buy in* from the oftentimes competing business, personal and political interests of all the parties involved. Mavericks excel at getting everyone to agree that a single solution—the

---

5   Sir Isaac Newton, *Philosophiae Naturalis Principia Mathematica* (1687).

Maverick's solution—satisfies all of their best interests as well as the good of the company. What follows is an example of an opportunity lost when a non-Maverick did not work the sale from all angles:

Frank and I meet for a quick beer after the end of the quarter, and I wanted to see how his new job was coming. Frank was at the bar when I arrived, and he did not look like the guy I had always known—he had forgone his beer in exchange for a martini. I pulled up a chair and asked how it was going. Frank explained that he lost a large deal to a smaller competitor, and he was not sure why. I asked what he heard from his contact within the account. His champion Ted was shocked that his manager went with the smaller company. Ted had done the evaluation and had recommended Frank's product. Frank shared that he was so confident in what Ted was doing that he did not feel the need to meet with anyone else. Ted was so enthusiastic about the product and would give glowing feedback that it seemed like a waste of time talking to others within the organization. Ted had said that he was the sole decision maker and did not need anyone else's approval or buy in. Ted felt that his manager did not understand the issues, even during the first presentation and demo, and did not ask any questions. I sat at the bar thinking to myself that if I was competing against Frank, I would go around Ted and meet with his manager one-on-one. Because I did not want to hurt Frank's feeling any more than they had been, I keep my thoughts to myself.

Understanding each stakeholder's needs and desires cannot be accomplished in a group setting. Mavericks ensure that they spend as much one-on-one time as possible with each of the players in the decision chain. Incidentally, this is preferably face-to-face time; phone and/or e-mail do not work as well because reading a buyer's body language and expressions is important for getting to the heart of his or her concerns. The Maverick's goal is to leave each person in the buying chain feeling confident that the seller is on his or her side: this leads to the win-win where everyone concurs.

The Maverick is rarely involved in a bake off without having met previously with all or most of the participants. Earning buyers' confidence—and Mavericks do earn it—does not happen in a group meeting and can never happen in a group situation where multiple vendors will be presenting their solutions. In a group setting, buyers present a united front of poker faces. The standard response to any seller's request for feedback in that setting will be "We'll get back to you on that."

Ideally, the first "official" meeting will not be a group meeting in which you have to deliver a blanket sales pitch to multiple decision makers with multiple agendas. In the best situation, you will be able to meet individually with key players without even the suggestion that there will be a large group meeting. However, if you cannot avoid a group meeting, do what Mavericks do: request a short informal tête-à-tête with each of the key decision makers ahead of the group session. This will give you an opportunity to get each person's unguarded point of view and learn how you can best address that person's concerns. Gathering this information prior to a group meeting gives you an opportunity to tailor your presentation to the individual agendas in the meeting. You will not have to worry about the united front, and you will set yourself apart from B Players who will go in hoping that their stock presentation will work for all stakeholders.

It Is Not the Product

The Bloomberg Terminal has 27,000 features that have all the bells and whistles, and yet not one of them differentiates itself from the rest. Not one. It is no longer enough to sell products; your product or service—which still needs to be great—is merely the ticket to the dance. It gets you in, but the modern buyer is not buying a product, he is buying solutions to his problem and business outcomes. Top sellers understand the competitive landscapes in which their prospects operate, and they know about innovations and standard practices in their targets' industries. These top sellers know their prospects' customers. Before the first sales call, Mavericks have scoured prospects' Web sites and other industry sources to get a firm grasp of the company's financials, reputation, market position, and prospects for the future. Mavericks do all this because they know that products are not at the top of customers' lists of business concerns. Results are what drives companies and are the focus of Maverick salesmen.

If you are relying or depend on your product and not your skill as a professional salesperson, then you are breaking this law. Often I hear salespeople state that if only their product had this feature or that feature, then they could sell. My comment to this is "So what? If you are dependent on the product to sell itself, the company would not need salespeople."

Mavericks routinely close sales using products that are not market leaders—or even well-known. They beat the competition by selling results that are best suited to their customers' immediate needs, and that anticipate their future needs. A Players keep their customers engaged in the sales process and confident that they made the best decisions for themselves and their companies. Engaged, confident buyers place Mavericks high on their list of vendors when they seek upgrades and enhancements or need solutions to other problems. The law of "It is not the product" puts the responsibility of selling were it needs to be—on the salesperson. Until you acknowledge that responsibility and take ownership of the sale, you will not reach your potential.

If You Know What's Going to Happen, Then You Know What to Do

This law is about applying your experience and ability to interrupt signals that the prospect is sending by taking corrective action before it is too late. The ability to anticipate what can go wrong and find a way to prevent it is the essence of this law.

In hindsight, everything is crystal clear: the unreturned phone calls, the slipped deadlines, and the prospect's less-than-enthusiastic response to a demonstration. In hindsight, when a deal falls through, the constant refrain from a seller is *"I knew that that was going to happen."*

Kevin and I had lunch, and he shared with me that his million-dollar deal had gone to our competitor. I asked what happened, and he said that they really liked our solution but kept asking us about our support for the ISO standard. Ken felt that he had responded appropriately and explained that we would have ISO support within the year. Ken shared that he had a sinking feeling that the deal was not going his way and stated that "he knew that this was going to happen." I was shocked and asked, "If you know it was going south, why did you not do something to stop it?" Kevin shared that he was just hoping that the issue would go away because it was a small issue that had no real business impact. I dug deeper and asked how long ago the client showed interest in this standard, and Kevin said that it was just after his competitor made their presentation. At that time, several people within the account brought up the idea of needing ISO support.

Mavericks refuse to sing this song because they do not take a wait-and-see approach to sales. Mavericks pay attention to the process and regularly ask themselves, "What's going to happen next?" and "What can go wrong?" Sometimes the answers are clear: the sales process is progressing the way that most of your successes have, and you know that it is smooth sailing until you close the sale. On the other hand, when the sale is not going exactly as planned, asking the aforementioned questions offers sellers the opportunity to resolve issues before these problems unleash a deal-killing blow. A Players get the answers to these questions by calling on past experiences, checking in with the prospect, and looking for previously unnoticed signs of trouble.

Listening to that internal voice that says, "Hey, I think something is wrong, and I think I need to do something about this problem," is a strong action taken by Mavericks. Waiting till that voice is proven correct is breaking this law. In your heart, you know that you are missing something and that either your competitor is cutting you off at your knees or there is a person within the account that you have misread.

You Know How to Sell, But Your Prospect Does Not Know How to Purchase

Although end users will insist that it only takes a few days to get a purchase order approved and signed at their companies, Mavericks know that this is not true. Very few people in an organization have extensive experience making major purchases in their companies, least of all, business and technical users. While their intentions are good, the fact is that there are very few occasions when a very large expenditure does not need multiple levels of approval. Complex buying goes through multiple levels of approval and review before a company proceeds. This is where A Players excel.

Jerry was frustrated with his new opportunity because the deal seemed stalled, and after several meetings with his champion, his promises of progress

had all turned into nothing but more "next steps." During coffee, I asked
Jerry what was his champion's role with the account. Jerry shared that he
was a very promising manager who is new to the group but really wants to
make an impact. I asked who else is behind the purchase of the product. Jerry
explained that the champion's whole team was on board. I quickly asked who
outside the champion's team was bought into the vision of what the product
could do for their organization. Jerry shared that the champion wanted to
manage that and did not want vendors contacting anyone outside his team.
I asked if the champion had purchased anything from anyone else before as
evidence that he would know the process. Jerry said that he had asked and
that he had not. Hum, I thought to myself. I remembered buying my first
house and all the issues that surrounded it, from mortgages to inspections
and closing costs. If it was not for my trusted real estate agent, I would
have made several very expressive mistakes. My realtor led me through the
prospect after understanding what I was looking for and could afford. The
realtor explained what I should expect and what to prepare for during the
transaction. Before going through the home-buying process, I really had no
appreciation for what realtors do and the value they provided, and I learned
that I did not know how to purchase real estate.

The end user has a job in the company, and buying is not their primary function. In fact, it is unlikely that buying anything other than routine office supplies is the job for any one person. That said, it is the seller's job to learn the process and be the shepherd for those making the buying decisions. This is the seller's job because part of making the sale is making the buying process easy. Once a prospect realizes that it takes more than "a few days" to get a purchase order approved, the process will stall. That is, the process will stall until a Maverick seller comes in and teaches the buyer how his or her company makes major purchases.

Set the Rules and Be Prepared to Change Them

In the best-case scenario, you are the first vendor that a prospect meets, which means that you can establish the rules. The rules present the criteria that the buyer should be looking for to make a sound purchasing decision. Remember: the buyer does not know how to buy a solution to his or her business problem. The Maverick uses those rules to make the case that his or her solution is the best one to meet the prospect's needs. While the Maverick is establishing the rules, he or she is also setting traps for their sales competitors. The Maverick's rules not only position his or her product as the best solution for the customer, but they also position the competitor products as poor options. It is not that competing solutions are inherently bad; rather, it is that those solutions do not meet the criteria set forth in the Maverick seller's rules. Therefore, the competing product will not satisfy the customer's needs.

For example, a Maverick will tell the customer that the best solution to his or her business problem is one that conforms to established industry standards. Such a solution would be compatible with technologies that the customer already uses and positions the company for smoother upgrades, future growth, and compatibility with soon-to-be-released peripheral products. Because the standard is so widely accepted, the buyer will have many options for training, support, and service. The rule, then, is that the customer should only consider using a standards-based solution, one of which the Maverick happens to be selling.

The rule also functions as a trap. The Maverick's competitor has a workable solution too. However, the competing product uses a proprietary technology. When the competition comes calling, and touting his product's innovativeness, the customer will already be of the mind that a proprietary solution limits his or her options for upgrades, growth, compatibility, and support.

On the other hand, even Mavericks cannot be the first vendors to talk to a prospect every time. In that case, the Maverick does two things. First, he or she determines the traps and rules set by the competition, and then the Maverick prepares well-crafted responses in his counter presentation.

Justin was competing for a new opportunity within the largest account inside his territory, and unfortunately, his competitor was the industry leader with the largest market share. I know Justin was a talented and experienced salesperson who had competed for large deals before and won most, but in this instance, the odds were certainly against him. When I had lunch with Justin to compare notes on each other's progress within our respective territories, he showed no sign of weakness about this opportunity but rather had a secret weapon that he felt confident would turn the tide his way. I asked looking for any new information I could. Justin shared that his large account was favoring a more stable and established vendor, but he had a feeling that responsiveness was also a characteristic that was highly valued. Justin explained that he made this the one and most important characteristic. He scheduled reference visits to other customers with whom he had worked successfully and had them explain how Justin had gotten the company to do back flips to meet new requirements and to have the product work with their unique situation. Justin provided good references on how he would be flexible and responsive to this company. In other words, he showed them just how important they would be to him and his company. Justin constantly built doubt about his competitor's ability to respond to unique needs and the clients need for on-site support with experienced consultants. I now understood why Justin is so successful.

To accomplish those two things, the Maverick seller does a side-by-side comparison of his or her product's benefits versus the competitors' offering. You can learn about a competing product's benefits and features by studying the company Web site. A side-by-side comparison gives the Maverick insight into how the competitor would have positioned the Maverick's product. The A Player takes the opportunity to reposition the competitor's strengths as weaknesses that the prospect should avoid at all costs. A few traps and rules that Mavericks use include as follows:

- **Standards.** If the competing product does not conform to industry standards, the Maverick will position that product as one that buyers will have trouble using outside of their own companies. If the product does not conform to standards, their partners and customers will be shut out. On the other hand, if the Maverick's product does not conform to an established standard, the seller may be able to prove that the existing standard is changing and that buyers will have a head start while their competitors are playing catch up.
- **Features.** Mavericks demonstrate how their product features serve their prospects' needs, while a competing product's features may not be as effective.
- **Integration with other products.** If a competing product does not integrate with buyers' existing product investments, it can be positioned as cost-prohibitive, forcing the buyer to replace their existing products as well.

- **Financial stability.** Being able to tout your company's financial position will cause prospects to examine your competitors' financial positions more closely. The last thing that they want is to be stuck trying to find support for a product developed by a company that has gone out of business.
- **Local support.** If your product can be supported locally versus a competitors' that may require shipping or waiting to have a technician flown in, your product will be a lot more attractive to prospects. Companies want to know that they will suffer a minimum amount of lost productivity should the product need servicing or if end users need technical support.
- **Market share.** Like financial stability, higher or increasing market share tells customers that your company will be around in the future.
- **Future product releases.** Customers want to know that your company is keeping up with advances in the marketplace. If your company has an aggressive release schedule, it will give them comfort that you will be able to keep up. On the other hand, a competitor's aggressive release schedule might be positioned as a negative: rapid deployments might indicate inadequate testing.

If you cannot establish the rules or change those that your competitors have set, you can encourage prospects to look at your weakest competitor. It is unlikely that the weaker competitor will win the business, but introducing another player could buy you extra time to strengthen your position.

Think about each of these laws and how they have worked in your sales. We will be referencing the law in the following chapter, and you will see how these work for the method and increase your level of success.

Chapter 4

THE MAVERICK SKILL SET

Since our focus is on the complex sale, and our target reader is someone who has several years of sales experience, we will not review the basic selling skills but rather focus on the skills that have separated Mavericks from the rest of the crowd.

The interpersonal sale also we will refer to as the simple sale. Additional selling skills are needed with the complex sale, for, with the complex sale, you are selling to a group of people but selling them in very different ways. So the interpersonal skills of building rapport, questioning, building interest, and closing are vital.

Defining the Complex Sale

It is important to define the type of sale that we are covering in this book. The complex sale has several characteristics. First, it involves selling to an organization, meaning that there will be several people and several groups playing some role in the purchasing decision. Second, the product is complex in many ways like the features and functions that can be beyond the knowledge of a single person.

The natural side effects of the complexities are that the complex sale takes a considerable amount of time, the cost of the product is high, and there are several competing alternatives to solve the problem.

With this understanding of the complex sale, it becomes clear that marketing will have limited ability to do anything more than create awareness. The complexity will also limit what the product can do on its own, unlike a simple sale where the marketing and product are dominant, and the sales function can be completed with classic selling techniques.

The complex sale will require an additional skill set, and we will describe what those skills are and what is needed, how they are to be applied and perfected. Think back to the deals that you have lost in your past: what did each have in common? Most likely they were deals where you were not sure what to do next, deals that had lost momentum, and deals that you certainly did not have control over. Now think of the deals that you have won over the years: these were deals where you knew exactly what to do next; they had momentum, and you were in control.

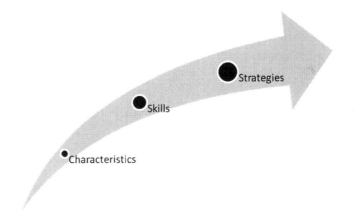

Now that we have outlined and described in chapter 2 the characteristics that make up and are necessary to excel in sales, we will build off those characteristics to the next level: skills. Since we are addressing the very best and most successful of salespeople, we are assuming that you have a strong understanding of the basic interpersonal selling skills like prospecting, qualifying, questioning, building interest, and closing. There are hundreds of books on interpersonal sales topics, and we feel there is no need to present them here. We would like to focus on the skills that take people from the A Player level and make them Mavericks. The skills that we will describe are all, again, targeted to the complex sale, and we will describe why the skills of the complex sale are different than those of the interpersonal sale. These skills are not hard to learn or to develop, but a surprising few are even aware of them.

"There are several meetings and evaluations and then something magical happens." I remember being in an interview with the founder and CEO of a well-founded start-up, and I was interested in understanding what their sales process was, and even though they did not have a product in the marketplace for long, they have closed several large customers. The CEO had been one of the key players in each of the deals, presenting his company's direction and explaining the commitment that they had for their first customers. With the CEO so involved in the sales process and in some cases being the leader of a particular deal, I felt that he would have a great deal of insight into how best drive the process. When I posed the question, "What is your sales process?" he responded very cavalierly, stating that there would be a series of meetings, presentations, and an evaluation phase. I then pressed and said, "OK, but how do you go from that evaluation phase to getting them to purchase?" And he got a little out of sorts and responded, "Well, something magical happens." I suspected that he may not have known but did not want to offend him, so I asked about the last deal in which he was directly involved in the closing. He explained that it was the last week of the quarter, and it was the only deal that was possible. He had flown in the night before and was aggressively pushing the CEO of the prospective customer for a purchase order. They spent the evening polishing their pitch and thinking over the objections. The CEO explained that the meeting went well, so I asked what the magic item was that made the deal happen. The CEO sheepishly explained that he offered a large discount and several days of free consulting. So that was the magic thing that happened? Yes, the CEO explained. *Well,* I thought to myself, *that is some process.* I'm sure that the CEO does not empower the sales force to generously discount and give away free services without executive review and approval.

Well, you will learn that you do not need any magic tricks to close complex deals in a timely and predictable manner. What this CEO and, frankly, 97 percent of the salespeople I know do not understand is that there is a decision path that organizations take when they purchase. That decision path can be shortcut with discounts and Hail Mary passes on the last day of the quarter, but if you know the path and develop the skills to control it, you can win the deal in a repeatable and predictable manner.

The complex sale is more than just a string of simple sales, and it is very dangerous to think of the complex sale as just a series of selling individuals because if you sell each individual without understanding his or her unique needs and vantage points, you will end up confusing instead of convincing. The complex sale will involve several people, all of whom who have their own agenda and their own view of what is good for the company and, more importantly, what is good for them. The complex sale deserves its name because there is no single decision maker; there are people who can veto a decision, but there needs to be consensus at some minimum level. Several of the characteristics of the complex sale make it difficult to build this consensus, including the time gaps between meetings and the lack of interest that certain stockholders will have for dealing with salespeople.

The skills that are needed to complete the complex sale are not taught by any sales training classes and are not addressed in any book. The necessary skills fall into three key areas: direction, momentum, and control.

Direction: Of course, everyone knows that you want to go straight to getting a purchase order, right? Yes, but how exactly does one get there? That is the hard part. Like my former CEO knew that there were presentations and a couple demos and even a lengthy evaluation process, but he did not know how to connect all that activity to getting the order. From his perspective, it was that magical meeting that was driven by his desperation to make a quarterly goal and to keep the board of directors from replacing him. The magical event was him buying the business with a lowball bid and supplementing it with free services. This is the norm and not the exception. The exception is knowing the process and the people involved in the process and mapping that out so that you know where you are and where you are going.

As in the physical world, when you want to go from point A to point B, you get a map that shows the routes and sometimes the terrain. How one actually gets from point A to B is up to the individual. The problem in the world of the complex sale is that since so few have been successful in navigating the terrain and routes, these paths are mostly in people's heads and not expressed on paper. It is true that most salespeople can list how they go from prospect to closure, but for anyone who has not been consistently successful in the complex sales, that list does not take into account enough detail or contingency to show someone else how to navigate it.

> *A good plan is like a road map: it shows the final destination and usually the best way to get there.*
> —H. Stanley Judd

The map to money, as we will refer to it in this book and will dedicate an entire chapter to it, is how the Maverick navigates the opportunities. The map to money is the big picture and the game board of the complex sale. There is good reason why no other sale book describes the map; it is because one rarely writes it down. The salespeople that I have studied have it in their heads and have built their strategies on top of it, but they do not take the time to document it.

Our clients often say we have tried the blue sheets or sales process models before and no one uses them. It is true there are several interpretations of documenting the sales process including war books, win plans, flight plans, and plan letters. We have never seen any organization really be successful by using any of them, although sales management has always been supportive of them. The reason these documents have failed over and over again is that they are not accurate representation of the terrain of the complex sale. They are a sequential list of actions and people, but they miss the key milestones, overlook what their competitors are doing, and fail to anticipate what can go wrong. At the individual level, these documents lack the individual style and strategy that each salesperson will employ. Without the individual salesperson buying into the process, the document just becomes an administrative artifact or check box item, and no real value is gained. These documents also do not take into account the unique characteristics of selling a particular product to a particular account.

The map to money is meant to cover the major components of the selling effort and is intended to be unique to both the product and the individual seller.

> *A cookbook must have recipes, but it shouldn't be a blueprint.*
> *It should be more inspirational; it should be a guide.*
> —Thomas Keller, Chef/Owner, The French Laundry

In the culinary world, the map is a recipe. A recipe is a list of ingredients and instructions to prepare a dish. A recipe makes the assumption that you have the basic skills and cooking utensils. The map to money has some of the same characteristics as a recipe in that there are general recipes that cover how to sell a particular product and make the assumption that the reader has basic selling skills and has access to selling tools. The recipe analogy is also applicable because skilled chefs will vary the recipe to their own abilities and tastes. The excellent chefs have also prepared dishes many times without referring to a written recipe; instead, they go from a kinesthetic state to create something that is unique to them.

Jerry was the most successful salesperson I had ever met at the time, and he was nice enough to spend time with me and help me understand what made a great salesperson. I would quiz him for hours about his deals and pull out of him what made him so successful. After several beers one night, he shared that what other salespeople do not understand is that organizations have two separate yet even important parts of the deal, the technical decision, meaning which product fits the functional requirements best, and the business decision, which product fits the overall economics of the company. Most salespeople, he said, become good at one or the other, but almost no one becomes good at both. Jerry said he figured this out early in his career and became good at both.

> *A relationship, I think, is like a shark, you know? It has to*
> *constantly move forward or it dies. And I think what we got on*
> *our hands is a dead shark.*
> —Woody Allen

Momentum: The momentum of a complex sale can be driven by the prospect, which is fine if it is moving at the pace that you are happy with, but it never is. Since the prospect is not trained in how to purchase your product, it is up to the salesperson to set and maintain the momentum of the deal. This skill is as rare as the understanding of the process and even rarer still as far as someone who can actually maintain the momentum without rushing the prospect or killing the deal.

How to build momentum:

Momentum is built by giving each player a strong personal reason to take action and to be part of that action. Applying the "divide and concur" natural law of sales will give you the opportunity to not depend on any one player but rather to build interest and gain insights from many different perspectives.

Dave had great momentum-maintaining skills, for he rarely ate a meal alone. Dave would find a good breakfast place close each of his target accounts and would invite key players to breakfast, and the busier people liked breakfast because it did not interfere with their schedule, and it was a nice way to get to know each other. Dave would never invite more than one person to breakfast, and he would match the restaurant to the individual he was inviting. Dave enjoyed the social aspect of meeting people off-site and would often wait for the prospect to bring up business as to not make people feel pressured or obligated to talk about business. Dave was able to build lasting relationships because he was focused on the personal wins that each person was looking for, and, in return, people would be great references for him. Dave knew that treating people to a meal was not in any way a new idea, but what was unique is that Dave did not just do it when he wanted information, he did it even when he did not have an agenda.

Once you have met the players, the simplest and yet most powerful way to build momentum is to create a reason for the next communication and settle on a time and date to communicate. This simple method will keep the ball rolling, and even if the next communication is a ten-minute phone call, it keeps the line of communications open and active.

Begin with the end in mind:

The prospect is purchasing a product to gain some business benefit; they want that benefit by some date, and it is that end date that will then drive every decision. So momentum must be built with that deadline in mind, and the action plan must be based on it. Once that deadline has been agreed upon, you now have the reason why every step must be completed by its own deadline and why each person in the process needs to communicate with you and keep the deal moving.

When you have momentum, you sense it, and it feels good. You are not pushing nor pulling; you are simply working together on a joint objective.

If you lose momentum, it is a very important sign that something is wrong, and your attention is needed immediately.

Control:

"Let's see what they have to say." This is what I hear most B Players say before a sales call. The B Players and even most A Players have no real control over the deal; they are simply responding to the prospect and asking what they would like to do next. What a Maverick does differently is to focus the prospect on what he or she wants to do next and leads the prospect through the buying process. Control is built from two attributes: being a leader and being proactive.

> *Leadership appears to be the art of getting others to want to do something you are convinced should be done.*
> —Vance Packard

Leadership is half of controlling the deal, for once you know where you are going, you need to lead your prospect through the process. Of course, they need to be willing to be led, which means you need to have added enough value to gain their trust. As the deal leader, it is you're responsibility to elicit each player's concerns and to answer their questions. Leadership is not relying on anyone else other than you to capture the deal. Leadership is not just moving the prospect from one step to the next but leading the prospect to what the decision criteria is and the rules that criteria is based on.

Being proactive is knowing what to do next and taking the actions to accomplish it. Being proactive is preventing what you know can go wrong and playing the game at least one move ahead.

Once you know where you are going, you need to know how you are going to get there and have enough momentum to arrive by the deadline you have set. How do you control the deal? The hardest and most advanced skill is controlling the sale. No one likes to be controlled, and, especially when you are paying money, the last thing you want is someone telling you what to do, but when we are in unfamiliar waters, we want someone to guide or even to lead us. So it is a key differentiator of the Maverick seller that he or she knows how to control the selling process without offending or alienating buyers or making them feeling controlled.

> *You can't control what you can't measure.*
> —Tom DeMarco

The direction that the map to money will give you and the momentum that we have created will require the *leadership* to control the deal.

Applying the natural laws of sales will give us the rules by which the game is played. The law that most apply to controlling the deal is this: You may know how to sell, but your prospect does not know how to buy. Once you internalize this law, you understand that it is the salespeople's responsibility to lead the sale; whether they take that responsibility or not, it is theirs. If you know what is going to happen, then you know what to do. By anticipating what is going to happen, both right and wrong, you are prepared to act and not just to react. By building these laws into your map, your thinking, and your strategy, it will become natural to understand why things happen the way they do and how you can control them.

How do you know if you are in control of the deal? You will know when you control by the way your prospect react to your requests. They will be asking for your help and support to justify their decision, they will be cooperative and confirming of your suggestions. Testing for control should be done with every communication by simply requesting an item of information or action and seeing if they comply.

Quid pro quo is the most powerful technique to control a deal. Once a prospect shows interest in your product, they will naturally request something from you, and this is where most salespeople miss the point. The natural response a salesperson has to a prospect's request is to immediately support the request with what they can give, which is the worst thing you can do because this the opportunity to get what you want, when you want it.

"Rogue Wave Case Study"

Rogue Wave Software ran into a growth challenge in 1998 when I first began working there. I noticed that the product pricing was on the Web site, which meant prospects did not need to call to get pricing, and, since they did not call, there was no dialogue. The result of the removal was that the number of inbound calls more than doubled. My role was a regional manager in what was the lowest performing region at the time. I wanted to first learn how things were being done, to see what could be done to increase revenue. I spent a week listening in on calls that the inside team would make, and I noticed that any time someone would ask for something, the sales person would jump to get it, which is great service but poor selling. When a prospect asks for something, it is a good time to ask for something in return; in fact, it is the perfect time to ask for something in return. The sales team expanded their use of quid pro quo to exchange evaluation copies for meetings, discounts for introduction to senior management and technical support for a deeper understanding of what they wanted to accomplish. The inside sales leaders were so impressed with what they were able to get with this selling skill that they coined the term "push back selling," and with this single skill, the team was able to dramatically increase the amount of control they had over each deal. Within two years, we were able to build the largest and fastest growing region in the company. So quid pro quo needs to be built into each interaction with the prospect, and the amount of preparation needs to be established so that you are matching their requests with getting the things you need. We have all experienced asking for something that we need, and if we do not have something to exchange, we are at the mercy of the prospect. We also know that the prospect will not be shy in demanding whatever they want to achieve of their own objective.

How to increase your control:

a. Determine what the prospect will be requesting at each milestone and be prepared to request one of three things in exchange for their request. A pattern will appear as to what the prospect will request at each of the touch points of the sales process, and it is important to know what they are going to be asking for and what you will need so that a fair and friendly exchange can take place. The smart thing to do is to ask for the largest and most viable item without overreaching so that the progress of the transaction can move forward.

b. The Maverick never gives the prospect anything without requesting something in return.

As salespeople, we feel obligated to give the prospect anything that they ask for, but in reality, we are really giving away our control of the process.

c. In the map to money, you will be having natural points where a request will arise and will need to have a prepared list of things that you will need to advance the deal.

We are not trying to say that these are the only skills nor are they the only ways that you can achieved direction, momentum, and control. We are only trying to explain what new skills and abilities are needed to be successful in the complex sale.

Chapter 5

CREATING THE MAP TO MONEY

No wind favors he who has no destined port.
                                        —Montaigne

The process map—which we'll perhaps rather coarsely call the map to money—is one of the simplest and least understood facets of the complex selling process. Indeed, it is generally the missing link in the sales process. Some sales strategists discuss the players and their buying roles or are just a list of milestones that need to be passed, but we've not yet come across anyone who develops a real map—a treasure map, if you will—that describes the exact number of steps between milestones and markers and landmarks and guides you to X: the treasure. The good treasure map will tell you which swamps have man-eating alligators and which just have annoying mosquitoes; it will tell you where there is quicksand and what to do if you get stuck in it; and it will point out any other potential traps and dangers. So will our map to money, a genuine treasure map.

Now it has to be said that A Players will be able to label the general things that need to be done to get a purchase order, but they will usually question prospects about what they'd like to do next instead of leading them through the map to money.

Without the map to money, salespeople are on what amounts to a wild-goose chase: they may occasionally catch a goose, but it is almost purely a matter of luck. Perhaps a better analogy would be a treasure hunt like that in the movie *National Treasure*. The hero has to unravel a set of mysteries, moving from one difficult clue to the next as he seeks the great treasure. At each step, our hero must be able to interpret correctly enigmatic poems (or signals) to determine his next move. Even our Maverick would find it challenging. The problem, of course, with hunting treasure without a good map is that it is reactionary; a salesperson without a good map has no control over the process and is prone to error when interpreting clues.

We've seen sales models that suggest the salesperson make a list of all the steps in the sales process and share it with the prospect. One trouble with this approach is that while many prospects are willing to help and even guide, they are rarely inclined to do the salesperson's job. Each has his prescribed role; lines should be respected and not crossed. We've actually tried sharing a list of the sales steps with prospects ourselves, only to watch the prospect roll his or her eyes and ignore the list. The main problem, of course, is that these lists tend to be linear; they go in sequence and are single-threaded and usually assume that one person can accomplish each item on the list.

That said, these lists can be a good starting point for developing a process map. Each item on the list needs to be matched to the correct player, and items that can be done concurrently (versus sequentially) need to be identified. What the map provides is a step-by-step visual representation of what needs to happen and what might go wrong, so that the seller can be ready with a response for all contingencies. It turns the treasure hunt into a treasure map, preparing the seller with the skills he will need, when he needs them, to be proactive in the sales process.

Incidentally, the map to money complements the law that states, "You know how to sell, but your prospect does not know how to purchase." The map provides the seller with a how-to guide from the buyer's perspective.

The main reason that sellers do not have a map in their minds, or as part of their strategy, is that maps takes a great deal of thought and reflection. Complex deals sometimes take more than a year to consummate. It is just natural—because it is easier—to take an action and then respond to the prospect's response to your action rather than try to envision the map, see the whole picture, and lead each player in the prospect company to closure.

"So What Happened?"

What happens, all too often, is that an introductory call is made to a kingpin account and the sales rep brings in the rock star presenter. Almost every organization has the guy who can share the vision better than anyone else; he most likely built the slide deck that all others use as the corporate standard. So the rock star presenter comes in all hyped up on coffee and goodwill. He builds the vision piece by piece, and the buyers connect with him, and he talks fast and loose with the facts and the state of the product. More often than not, the amount of time that was allocated for the meeting has expired, but there are still fifteen slides to go. The audience is still enthralled, but stomachs begin to grumble and another group needs the meeting room and other priorities of everyday work life begin to rear their ugly heads. The prospect apologizes, and the projector is taken to its next appointment. The sales team is ushered to the lobby, and it is all smiles and handshakes with the proverbial "let's talk soon" goodbye. The rock star from corporate is all too pleased with yet another standing ovation.

The salesperson makes a determination of forecast ability based on something that is simply not understood. In this case, Mr. Rock Star returns to corporate with stories of the brilliant conquest and assures the executive team that a huge win is imminent; it is all but closed. Of course, the salesperson follows up, offering a proposal and a contract for the prospect's lawyer to review and is met with a wall of silence. He gets the brush off. Corporate wants to know what happened and wrongly concludes that the salesperson somehow screwed up a slam-dunk deal. The salesperson is accused of incompetence and is let go.

Now you may be saying to yourself that it's so obvious: they didn't close for the next meeting, or they somehow misread what the prospect wanted or needed. Both are right. But these problems are endemic and do not just affect the rookie, but the twenty-year veteran as well. Generally, it is the difference between the B Player and the Maverick: the B Player is reacting to the whims of the prospect rather than leading the prospect through a process to a business decision.

The money map is necessary because it is simply too much to ask for a salesperson to master all the selling skills, integrate them into his personality, and then apply them in the field. The only logical solution is to break down the process into its component parts: understandable parts that can be learned and practiced so that, once in the field, the salesperson can know what to do and how to do it.

You will find that each product and salesperson will have a unique map to money, with very different characteristics and skills that will be needed to move the process forward to the goal. Mavericks may not draw it or have an artifact that they call a map, but it is in their head and wired into their DNA. Without this map, salespeople are hunting and pecking, trying to find their way to closing a deal.

The biggest blank spot on most maps to money is between the first call and the business win (terms we shall define in a moment). So often, the salesperson does not even understand what mechanically happens in this process, never mind having any control or leadership through the process. The B Player generally has a pretty good handle on the first call—the first landmark on the map—and on the back end process of dealing with purchasing. But he generally falls apart in the middle: controlling the process of the decision and the allocation of the budget.

Let's look now at the key facets of *every* sales call:

- What is the objective of the call?
- What are they going to ask for? What are three things that I will ask for in return?
- How will I know if we can move forward? What is the next forward movement?
- What has our competitor been doing?
- What is the next touch point that we can get agreement on?

Below is a very general outline of the sales process or map to money. Note that the first two arrows on the left are not straight lines but rather a bit convoluted. So is the process. And remember, this is the blank spot and the most difficult terrain on most maps to money.

First Call

The first call is typically a meeting arranged through effective prospecting that has won a salesperson a seat at the table. The objective of the first call is to find out who the stakeholders are and to turn the person with whom you are meeting into an ally: a guide at worst and an advocate at best. The advocate not only tells you what's going on, but also takes you to the economic buyer, which is the desired outcome of the first call: an introduction to the economic or business buyer, the person who controls the purse strings.

Meet with Each Stakeholder Individually

In that wasteland between the first call and the business win lies, among other potential traps, meetings with each of the stakeholders individually. The purpose of these meetings is to find out what each person needs—be it financial, political, or economic—and work out how you can meet those needs.

Technical Win

Salespeople tend to be optimistic. Imagine a fifteen-year-old going into a Porsche dealership. He knows everything there is to know about Porsches. He knows just what he wants: year, make, model, color, and interior, even custom stereo system. The salesman is all excited (of course, unaware of the child's minority) and begins to draw up the paperwork. Just then the boy's father comes in and, a bit perturbed, says, "Son, we're already late for practice—get in the car."

The technical win is the winning over of the end user of your product or service. The technical buyer, like the fifteen-year-old Porsche shopper, does not have decision-making authority. He cannot write the check. He must take you to the economic—or business—buyer.

- The *technical win* is defined as the selection of the solution to the exclusion of all other alternatives to solve their business problem.
- Establish that there is something that needs to be solved.

- Become a possible solution.
- Become the preferred solution.
- Lock out the alternative solutions.

Business Win

The business win occurs when the economic sale takes place. The business buyer, by contrast to the technical buyer, can write the check. Of course, he is likely to take you to the technical buyer to see if your product actually works. He has political, financial, or user experience, but not usually technical experience.

Too often, the business win is not begun until the technical win is secured. This is far too late and leads to false deals and deals that take longer and become smaller. The technical win is largely worthless without getting the business win. The business win should begin at the same time, and the selling should continue concurrently.

The business win is harder because the business players do not know why they are dealing with you—because they haven't made a decision to select you yet. *Quid pro quo* should be used as the method to be introduced to the person who will sponsor you from a financial standpoint. A relationship will need to be established with each of the people who will need to approve the purchase, and in each case, they will need to know why they are approving this option in comparison to all the other alternative solutions to their problem. The key mistake is not working this angle from the beginning—is not learning the language of the businesspeople. Businesspeople focus on the operations and leadership issues; they care about revenue, expense, and the competitiveness of the business and want to know how this purchase will affect these areas of the business. They do not care about the bells and whistles of the product. They do not want to see demos, but they do want to learn about your company's suitability as a business partner. And they care about testimonials from other companies that have used your product.

- The *business win* is defined as the decision to purchase because it makes business sense and the prospect sees the end vision.
- Use the business sale to jointly develop a business justification.

- Determine the funding authorization level needed to approve the deal.

Legal

The legal aspect of a sale is a technicality: the bulk of the hard work has been done. This is a matter of crossing the *t*'s and dotting the *i*'s and agreeing on a legal contract that can be passed on to purchasing.

Purchasing

There may be some negotiation of terms left to do, but if you have sold properly, the negotiations should go largely in your favor. In the sale of an innovation or disruptive technology, there are, by definition, no competitors. The product is quite literally unique in the marketplace. But there is always competition with other uses of money or with internal solutions.

Sales Cartography

Making maps to money (the set of steps and milestones that sellers must achieve in order to sell innovative or disruptive products or services) seems to be an art lost with the pirates of yore. Sales mapmaking is a skill rarely if ever taught; many models treat the organization as a single person rather than as a group of disparate individuals with different needs and different desires. These other models also tend to focus on reacting to a prospect's requests rather than leading the prospect step-by-step to the purchase.

The Maverick establishes a map to money early and quickly and leads the prospect through the process rather than depending on what the prospect wants to do next. (Prospects, more often than not, do not know what they want to do, and even when they do, they often do not know how to do it.) You need to know where you are going if have any hope of getting there.

Then it doesn't matter which way you go, said the Cat.
—Lewis Carroll, *Alice in Wonderland*

I am told there is a passage in the Talmud that says as follows: "If you don't know where you are going, any road will take you there."

A Few Key Insights Will Keep the Momentum

1. Knowing what can go wrong at each stage of the selling process allows you to prepare for it and prevent it. The things that go wrong are consistent, and overconfidence is the biggest obstacle. Take preventative measures and have a plan to recover from anything that might go wrong.
2. Knowing what the owner of the alternative solution might do to derail the progress of the decision is a key foresight. You can set traps to lock competitors out.
3. Define the cadence of contact with each of the key players. Control and drive the process by keeping a cadence of communications with each of the key players in the account.
4. Set and hold a deadline that must be reached, and everything will be driven from this deadline.

Each milestone is important and needs to be understood properly. For instance, how do you know when you've achieved the technical win or any of the other milestones? What will your competitors do once they know you have achieved a milestone? Remember, competitors in the space we're discussing (innovative or disruptive products and services) are competing for wallet share, but they are not competing on product or service because your offering is truly unique in the marketplace. Let's be crystal clear: innovative and disruptive technologies are not incremental improvements; they represent a new paradigm altogether. The next question is this: how do we lead the prospect to the next step?

Also, what happens if you lose at a particular milestone? Do you give up and walk away? By no means. There are several tactics that can be employed to recover from a perceived loss. You can try an end run to a higher power (not in the Bill W. sense); you can muddy the waters with the weakest competitor.

The Rhythm to Revenue

Like everything else in life, a deal has a rhythm and a pace that need to be identified and followed. It is the salesperson's responsibility to lead the pace and to become concerned when the pace is broken. The rhythm needs to be established with each of the key players within the organization. Some characteristics of the rhythm include the following:

1. The "let's talk next week" factor by which you establish regular contact with the key players.
2. Commitment to the next touch point needs to be voluntary and mutually agreed upon.
3. If the rhythm is broken, it is a negative signal that needs to be addressed posthaste.
4. When a next touch point is not committed to, then you know that you do not have interest, and you do not have an opportunity. Walk away.

The Rules by Which a Solution Will Be Selected

The rule is "It is not the product." Who is it that sets the rules for selecting one solution over another? Well, it is usually whoever has the most compelling reason for selecting one versus the other. The C Player always blames the product, his company, the customer, and anything or anyone but himself. It is the salesperson's job to define the reasons why a customer ought to buy his solution versus any other. If it were a pure matter of product superiority, then the superior product would always be selected, and there would be no reason to have more than one product for a market segment. But it is not the product; it is a collection of perceptions that are dynamic and changeable by talented Mavericks. Think about the recency effect (the principle that the most recently presented items or experiences will most likely be remembered best): viewers of two talented debaters will often flip-flop in their thinking each time the speaker changes. In the complex sale, what matters is not only what you are saying, but also who you are saying it to and how often you are saying it. The rules by which decisions are made include such data points as the following:

1. Priorities
2. Values
3. Perceptions

A lockout is something only your solution has or does; beware of traps and remember the old saying: He who sets the rules wins the game. Set the rules.

The Power of Why?

People will only do what they have a strong reason to do. So it is the salesperson's responsibility to establish the way for each of the players. It is also his responsibility to keep reminding them why they are buying, so he will always be prepared to give an answer to everyone who asks him to give the reason for the hope that is within him.

1. Each person needs to know why they are purchasing.
2. Each person's reason can be different.

The Players

The man. Too often, salespeople require a champion—or advocate—to do a lot of the selling for them. Having a champion is great, but you cannot sell *only* to prospects that provide you with a champion! Moreover, you need to know how to sell *with* them, not under them. It is generally from the technical side of the house that you will find your helper. There is a continuum of support on the technical side of the house, and it is vital that it be understood.

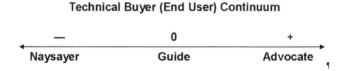

Technical Buyer (End User) Continuum

The end user, or technical buyer, needs to be brought, at very least, to zero. The positive end of the spectrum ranges from guide to advocate. So just exactly who are all these people? And who are the other players?

The naysayer. The naysayer is the person who is going to block and kill the progress of the deal. He is generally the person who will lose power if your solution is selected. It is the person who feels it is his job to slow things down, and he feels that he must change the vision to add value. You don't need to make a naysayer into an advocate, but you need him to be neutral. Don't try to win him over—be satisfied with neutralizing him. Bring him to zero.

The guide. The guide is not necessarily a great partner, but he is willing and helpful—as much as he can be. He likes what you have to offer and sees the value of it—but he's not going to stick his neck out too far.

The advocate. The advocate not only tells you what's going on, but also takes you to the economic buyer. He is your partner in the sale. Whatever his reason, he wants the sale to happen as badly as you do. He helps identify the milestones, the rules, and the players. He translates company-specific language for you and provides insight into what the end vision must look like. He conscientiously warns of pitfalls and gives insight into the alternatives and what competitors are doing.

The problem owner. This is the business group leader who owns the problem that the Maverick is trying to solve. He may not initially be aware of the pain he is suffering. How do you get him to become aware of the pain that you can salve?

The budget owner. This is the person who will ultimately exchange money for a vision of the solution. How do you build up the value versus the cost? He will need a documented business justification. He is the one with whom you must share the bright and shiny vision of a future paved with gold. He cries out for a visionary type of presentation. What is the end business result that will justify both the cost and the effort of making the change? The bigger and brighter the vision, the more it is worth. Extend the vision beyond the current functionality. You need to get them to buy into not only what the product will do for them, but also how the business result will change them.

Selling Without a Champion

We did not overlook the champion. With most descriptions of the complex sale, there is always a reference to a player who has a champion or someone who does a great deal of the selling for you. Some salespeople even go as far as saying that without a champion, no one will be successful. We all know that when you have a champion, the process is a great deal easier, but a champion is not a necessity for someone who understands the process.

It is actually very dangerous to depend on any one individual regardless of his or her level of interest. Mavericks are their own champions, know the path that the decision will take, and build up the consensus of all the players.

Signals

In sales, we are always evaluating what is happening within our prospect's account and what the true feelings are of each of the players. Too often, sellers go by what is being verbalized by the players and ignore what is being left unsaid. The most accurate representation of what is really happening comes from the signals or actions that are being taken. The signals must be learned as quickly as possible, especially if you are losing to a competitor or to "no action required."

To control the process, you need to work with accurate information and current information, so learning about and watching for signals is crucially important.

Positive signals. The following signals need to be validated to make sure they are true:

- Anytime they meet a commitment.
- They ask for justifications, either technical or financial.
- They include you in internal meetings.
- They provide introductions to others.
- They share impressions of the competition.

Negative signals.

- Mostly questions about an alternative's strength/traps/lockouts.
- The communication cadence is broken.
- Unexpected milestones are added.
- The advocate is losing credibility.
- The advocate's information is not helping.

What are the signals that are unique to your product?

Integrity scale. Tracking each player's integrity will give a way of gauging each interaction with him or her. Examples of such tracking include the following:

- How accurate is their information?
- Are they on time?
- Do they keep cadence with you?
- Are they selling you?

> The power of the map to money is not in creating a mandated corporate process but in marking the pivotal milestones and decision points. Once you identify the pattern by which organizations determine to buy your product, you can match your skills to build your own unique strategy. It also needs to be said that your map is yours and can be on paper, built with a software application, on a whiteboard, or even in your head. The format of the map does not matter: the use and content of the map do matter. Without the map, your journey is touch and go, so—at minimum—think the process through and work with your peers to determine the best approach to each and every issue.

With long sales cycles and managing many opportunities, it is easy to become rusty or even neglect particular skills. The map gives you a quick refresher to the issues and variables that you are facing. Many people tell us that after closing a large deal, they feel like a fish out of water because they have not prospected in three to six months. The map gives people a feeling of leverage in that they do not have to recreate the wheel but simply build off their experience of success and learn from their failures.

> The typical representations of a complex sale only categorize the players or list the milestones of a deal. The map to money documents the whole picture and allows the individual to match the terrain to his or her skills. The fact is that, without the map, we are relying on gut instinct and instinctive skills. With the map, there is a clearly defined process that has been proven to work.

Chapter 6

THE FIRST SALES CALL

Everyone knows the emotional energy and angst that goes into a first date. Anyone who dated before the advent of online dating understands what the nervousness and threat of rejection does to an otherwise even-keeled person. Recall the difficulties you encountered on the first meeting when your gut told you that your date was not very interested in you. At that moment, you realized that it was all up to you to convince your date how great a person you are. Before the date, you rehearsed everything in your mind, wrote "talking points," prepared your funniest stories, and chose the coolest unknown place that would be a hit for your date. Well, the first sales call is very much like those first dates in more ways than we would like to remember. We all know that if we do not connect on the first date, our follow-up calls will go unanswered or we will be stonewalled with alternatives similar to the old standby "I need to wash my hair on Saturday night."

The first face-to-face sales call is much like a first date, and it is so important because too often it is the last sales call. The first call is the hardest because it requires the most preparation, the prospect cares the least, and most of the deal-killing mistakes take place. We spend a great deal of time on the first call because without a qualified and documented success, salespeople may be misled into believing everything is moving forward when in truth, all they have is an illusion of a successful meeting. That illusion gives the salesperson a comfortable feeling for weeks and months until the day that he/she realizes there is nothing.

Does it seem logical that someone would spend weeks working on getting the first meeting with a company and, once the appointment is made, only spend a few minutes preparing for the meeting? No, of course not. But that is what many do—they rationalize it by saying, "Hey, lets see what they have to say." The other problem is people spend too much time practicing their slide deck, collecting information packs but do not develop a strategy to describe the problems that their product solves.

> In sales, like structural engineering, there is "the Chain Link syndrome." This is the description that was given when I worked for a company ironically named Chain Link Technology, and the VP of sales described what happened after the first sales call. You could swap out the name Chain Link for pretty much the name of any company, and it would fit into the "syndrome." The syndrome was simple: an aggressive salesperson would gain access to an account and build enough interest to schedule a meeting. The salesperson armed with a talented and prepared domain expert would arrive for a briefing. The presentation would go flawlessly with several wows and ahs. The demonstration of the product would be received with great enthusiasm. The meeting would go far past the ninety minutes that were allocated, and the sales team would leave and give each other high fives in the parking lot, knowing that they have knocked it out of the park and that this was now a forecasted deal. The salesperson would follow up with a timely call one week after the meeting to confer and ask what they would like to do next. Unfortunately, the call and subsequent e-mails would go unanswered, and it seemed as if they had never had the meeting in the first place. So what went wrong? The prospect was clearly interested and amazed at the presentation, but yet the idea died in the client's hands, and the sales company felt like this

was something that had never happened before in the annals of business. So rare was the event that they called it a *syndrome* and warmed all new salespeople that this is something that can (and will) happen. Well, was it unusual, or was it the result of a lack of a sales process?

This *syndrome* is not a mystery to those who understand Maverick salespeople and the difference between a complex and simple sale. What was missing from this aforementioned sales call was a way to connect to the next milestone in the decision path. Did the salesperson give each person a reason as to why his/her lives would be better because of the product?

You may be saying to yourself that it is so obvious they did not close for the next meeting or sense what the prospect wanted or needed. These problems are classic and effect the rookie as well as the twenty-year veteran. Mostly it is a case of separating the difference between the B and A Player. The B Player is reacting to what the prospect wants versus leading the prospect through the process of making a business decision.

Similar to the first date, if you do all the talking, the date (or in this case the client) may be entertained but get lost in the meeting because you come across as self-centered. Maybe the opposite could work. Maybe by having questions that would show interest in the other person and his/her needs, you would get insight into his/her needs and areas of common interest.

The objective of the first call is to determine first if the account is qualified, meaning that there is a need/pain that can be identified and built upon. From that point, you have something that can be developed and matched to what your product does. Much like the first date, you want to learn if you are interested in more than what you already know, which may just be an appearance. The balance of finding out what you want to know without offending or being transparent becomes the challenge.

The first call can come about in several ways, including a response to either a cold call or request for information from the prospect. We will separate the first calls into two main kinds: a push, when the salesperson makes an initial phone call to build interest, and the second type being a pull, when the prospect has expressed interest in learning about the product.

Let us use the situation of a cold call where you are pushing to meet with the prospective client. This call, like all calls, is best delivered one-on-one where you are looking to magnify the pain that they have and that your product solves. Once you have determined that the account is qualified, meaning that they have the need, you must ensure that they are participating and have the financial resources to complete a transaction. The need can be either discovered or undiscovered, but at the end of the meeting, without the need/pain, there will not be a deal. In the rare exception, there is a deal without a need; this results from someone cramming the product into an unnecessary place where it will just collect dust, possibly engender bad will, and create poor future business relations.

When it is a pull call, meaning that the prospect is looking for a product and yours is one of the possible choices, this would seem like an easier sale. In truth, what is really happening is that they have asked three or more of your competitors to demonstrate products, and this becomes a dogfight to see who wins. The prospect clearly views you as just one of many, so the job is to determine their real and perceived needs and to have your product and company match them to a significantly higher degree than your competitor's product or approach.

The prospect that contacts you with a pull call is not going to be a key player. Most often, this contact is simply there to orchestrate the meeting and administrate the logistics, so you will need to push to get a face-to-face prep meeting so that the presentation will be a success. The person calling you is going to view your request as a hassle, so quid pro quo is the best approach as exemplified below.

The best execution of the quid pro quo is to agree with the prospect and say, "Yes, we look forward to making the presentation to your team, and before we schedule, may I have a ten-minute conversation with XXX." In this case, XXX is the lead technical person on the meeting team. You do not want to make the quid pro quo a condition; rather, it becomes simply a part of completing what the prospect has requested.

If they refuse your request, you can see this as a *signal* that you are not a critical option for their choice. Of course, you do not want to walk away, so an alternative strategy may be to do some networking and research to find the key technical player and contact them directly using someone else from your company so as to not be seen as someone end-running the process.

Once you are able to get the prep meeting, it should be casual and one-on-one so that you can gather as much information as possible about their situation (need/pain) and the end goals. You want to be sensitive to traps that your competitors have set and what would be in the key technical decision maker's best interest.

Once you have your presentation set, request a meeting with the key technical decision maker after the call to talk about providing some kind of value to him. This will be a key time to get their feedback.

Of course, the key test of how well the meeting has gone is if you receive a commitment for the next meeting. Of course, confirming the next meeting should be done one-on-one in order to avoid the "We will get back to you" canned response.

The most important law that applies to the first sales call is that if you know what is going to happen, then you will know what to do. If your presentation and demonstration takes two hours, and you only have an hour and a half, you will need to schedule two meetings (which is a good thing). Having met with a great deal of junior salespeople and questioning them about their first calls, you hear the same thing over and over: "It went great, and they really got it." My next question, asking when the next meeting is scheduled, often elicits the same response—"They asked me to check back in a couple of weeks"—and it is at this point that I realize this junior salesperson does not fully understand the process.

Let us remember the "Chain Link syndrome" or should we call it the first and last sales call syndrome. A great presenter can capture people's interest, but without identifying the need/pain and leading the prospects to understand how the product's capability will ease the pain, there is no compelling reason for the prospective client to move forward to a next meeting. If you know the prospect is not willing to commit to a next meeting or communication, you can be confident that you will not have a deal.

So if you know what is going to happen, let us talk about what we should do to make the good things happen and the bad things not.

The Maverick has a brutal sense of self-evaluation regarding where they stand in a deal and go so far as to set up acid tests for each position. The acid test for determining if you passed the first call is if the prospect commits to the next meeting or not. This momentum test is talked to death in this book, but it is the most powerful test of where you stand. It is just too easy to say, "Thanks for meeting with us," and "I will call you next week." This is a cop-out, and what is missing is the salesman giving them a need for them to return your call next week. The close for the next communication is in a sense asking them what is in the way of us moving to the next step. An important note is that if the account is not qualified, you certainly do not want to spend any more time or commit to a next meeting. If the prospect cancels your next meeting without quickly rescheduling, your deal is suspect at best.

It may be sexist but I must venture to say that women are much more evolved in this area of keeping the momentum of dating. Often I would find items left in my car or apartment after a date and thought naively that I was attracted to only forgetful young ladies. When I shared the story with a female friend, she enlightened me to the old "leave your gloves" strategy. Leaving gloves had nothing to do with being forgetful, but rather a great reason to call and arrange for another meeting to return the gloves. These young ladies would make good salespeople because they know how to keep the game in play.

The Good Things:

Your product is seen as the best match.
They have committed to a next meeting or communication.
You have set traps for the competitors that will present after you.
They have asked for something, and you have quid pro quo for something.

The Bad Things:

They did not understand the value of your product, or as many say, they did not "get it."
You walked into a competitor's trap and could not get out.

They loved the presentation but did not commit to a next meeting.

You could not get one-on-one time with the key players.

You missed the signals.

Did not identify the pain or they did not see how you solved their pain.

Another law to remember when working on the technical win is that the first call is not about the product. It is the art of identifying the pain that the prospect is experiencing that leads to setting the rules as to how the problem will be solved. The product is the crutch that the junior salespeople depend on and blame for all the bad things that happen. Mavericks take full responsibility for the deal, and by doing so, it opens their minds to all the elements.

What to do after the meeting?

Unlike a date, your sales calls affect your income and level of career success, so they need a higher amount of examination and review.

"The Postmortem"

Early in my career, I had the honor of working with a team of senior salespeople who were extremely successful and talented. One of their habits was to have what they called a postmortem after each face-to-face sales call. They would pick the meeting apart and write out the new information that they found and update the organizational chart with changes of what they had discovered. This exercise was a way to continue building and refining their "map." They would compare how this deal was working to several of the deals that they had done in the past. They would rank each of the players as to whether they were positive, natural, or negative to the product. Working together as a team, the group would play a type of war game by asking what would happen if the sales group did either x or y and debating the best actions to take.

I learned more in those postmortem meetings than I have in any training class. By thinking through the issues and possible actions, the sales team could have a plan that everyone accepted.

After I left this company, I was surprised to learn that other salespeople do not do this activity and even more surprised to learn that several salespeople thought it was worth the time saying that they will either buy or they will not. I learned that even salespeople with fifteen or twenty years of experience would not develop themselves beyond the interpersonal selling skills level and did not have a strategy. They would rely on their bubbly personalities or hounding the prospect until they simply gave into their demands. However, as the sale becomes more and more complex, the skills are simply not enough; salespeople need to understand how the decision is going to be made, develop a strategy to convince each of the players that the decision means selecting your product and it is worth substantial more than the money that they are paying.

After the meeting, as soon as possible, you need to sit back and review what took place. Replay their questions and the interaction that took place between the players. Use a sign in sheet to make sure you have everyone's contact info and who was interested in what items. Label the player that seemed smart, interested, and asked questions. The sign in sheet is the most important artifact from the first call because without it, you may have business cards, but not everyone brings business cards, and the information on them is often dated, making follow-up difficult.

Another smart move is to leave a couple of questions unanswered for the simple purpose of justifying a follow-up call. Again, if they are not interested in scheduling a time to get the answers to their questions, then you do not have a deal, and that is what we call a signal.

The next law to apply is divide and "concur." If this is a pull call, it becomes harder to apply divide and concur because you are not talking to a problem owner or a player with power. The person you are talking to simply wants you to commit to a presentation.

After the first call, "divide and concur" with each person who was at the presentation. The different insights that you will get from each will be valuable and will enable you to build a picture of what to do next and how to accomplish the tasks.

Think about how the law of divide and "concur" would work in the dating world. Would you really want to take your first date to meet your family or friends? Imagine managing your date's impression of you with your mother showing pictures of you in the bathtub when you were two years old or your friends sharing stories of your college years. Even worse, imagine having to be with friends of your date who would all be qualifying you for how you would fit into their social circle. From this example, it becomes clear that convincing people is always most effective one-on-one.

After the first sales call, you will be able to identify the key players including who is the most important and who is responsible for making a recommendation to the business problem owner, whose opinion matters most and who are the naysayers.

How to determine if you are prepared for the first sales call:

Do you understand with whom you are meeting and what they know about your product so far?

What other customers do you have that have already done what your target prospect wants to do?

Have you done Internet research on the company and the person with whom you are meeting?

— How can you apply what you have learned from your research to make the call more applicable to the prospect's situation?

What are the typical things that the prospect wants from you and your company if the meeting goes well?

What are the corresponding items that you can get in exchange?

What traps may have been set for you by your competitors?

What lockouts can you use to limit the impact your competitors may have?

Chapter 7

THE TECHNICAL WIN

Any sufficiently advanced technology is indistinguishable from magic.
—Arthur C. Clarke

The technical win is important but not critical in the complex sale. It is defined as the selection of the innovative or disruptive solution to the exclusion of all other alternatives to solve a business problem. It is the winning over of the end user, the functionality evaluator who will actually have to use the new product or service to meet a real need. The good news is that many technicians are also technologists who love technology for its own sake, and they find themselves willing to adopt new technology just because it is so very cool. The bad news is that they don't hold the purse strings.

There are three states of the technical win: favorite, neutral, and not the favorite. The sublime state of favorite is the only one in which you will be given positive reinforcement and, therefore, the only state you will know for sure that you are in. Whether you are in neutral state or precisely not the favorite, you won't know—so your job is, at least, to neutralize anyone who has not given you positive reinforcement. Each state requires a different strategy because they are all open to change and manipulation.

The Mechanics of the Technical Win

Favorite

The purpose of the technical win is to create a smooth path to the business win. It will also make implementation much easier if you have the technicians on your side. There is no magic bullet for the technical win; it takes hard work. If you are selling an innovative or disruptive product or service, you are apt to meet with natural resistance. People fear the unknown. They have ever since the earth was flat and it was possible to sail off the end of it. Fortunately, as we pointed out, many technical buyers are apt to be technologists who love innovation qua innovation. You must generally convince your audience, the technical buyer, first, that he has a need and, second, that you can solve it—albeit in an unorthodox fashion. So the steps through the technical sale are as follows:

1. Establish that there is something that needs to be solved.
2. Become a possible solution.
3. Become the preferred solution.
4. Lock out the alternative solutions.
      Favorite status, incidentally, does not allow you to rest on your laurels—there is still yeoman's work to be done, which brings us to the most important item:
5. Secure an introduction to the business buyer—the earlier in the process, the better.

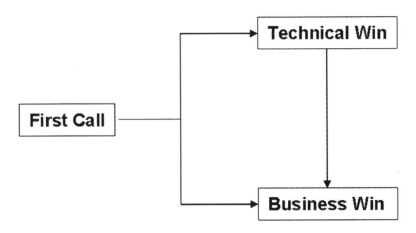

Establish that there is something that needs to be solved

This is not always as easy as you may imagine. With an incremental improvement, selling efforts are focused on the *product*: "This is so much better, faster, handsomer, etc." And the more familiar the customer is with the competition, the more obviously it is just an improvement (an extraordinary improvement, notwithstanding). The problem is that, with an innovation, selling efforts need to be focused on the *experience*. A new paradigm is often so far out of the prospect's frame of reference that, unless you are dealing with a serious technologist, the technology by itself will make no sense. Imagine what it was like trying to sell an automobile in the early days: You could really sell it only as a hobby for the wealthy because there were no roads and people didn't understand the concept of machinery for leisure—machinery was for work.[6] So selling a car (versus the horse and buggy), you would have had to focus the (potential) customer on the *experience*. "Do you ever have to be somewhere at a specific time? What happens when it's raining and muddy? What happens when your horse throws a shoe?" You needed to keep bringing them back to the *experience*—not the technology.

So it is in the modern age when you are dealing with a paradigm shift: you must focus on the *experience*, not the product. Therefore, you have to frame the conversation with a problem that the end user probably doesn't even know he has. You have to convince him that there is a better way to do things and that the current way of doing things is fraught with *future* peril. You are here to save him from *future* disaster. It is in many ways a powerful skill. It comes back to painting a picture, sharing a vision of what the future could be—both positive and negative.

Become a possible solution

Once the technical buyer sees the vision and accepts that there could be a problem, you need to show him that your technology is

---

[6] *Horsepower*: 1806, from *horse* + *power*, established by Watt as the power needed to lift 33,000 pounds one foot in one minute, which is actually about 1.5 times the power of a strong horse.

a practical (compared to the looming danger), relatively low-cost solution. He needs to understand that your wares will, in fact, meet the case and are a legitimate potential solution.

Become the preferred solution

Having established that there is a very real problem and that you have a possible solution, you must convince your technical buyer that you are, in fact, the preferred solution. You have an advantage in that yours is the only product in the running. But there will be competition from the status quo, and there will be competition for a share of the wallet from those who can meet today's immediate needs. Continue to build value by focusing on the experience—wouldn't it be nice to be able to visit your neighbors twenty miles away in one hour rather than two?

Lock out the alternative solutions

Competing ideas will arise, although there are no competing products—not for what you are selling.

The lockout is that particular characteristic that is unique to your product or company. An industry standard, for example, or a patent or a functional characteristic or support capability—these are lockouts. It is that characteristic that distinguishes you, sets you apart (and above), which cannot be replicated by any other. It effectively locks out the competition. It is a very powerful strategy because it gives the customer a reason to select you, and you avoid having to compete on the myriad of other issues. Many salespeople are concerned that their lockout will not matter to the customer—but the point is that, even if it doesn't matter now, it will, in fact, matter in the future. You need to beware of one thing. In negotiations, it is called argument dilution: The lockout loses its power if it does not stand alone. Do not bring up a number of lockouts (even if they are all legitimate); it dilutes the power of your argument. Choose the one that will have the most impact and that best matches the prospect's particular situation. If the lockout is a technical lockout, it is important to map it to a business value so that once you are capturing the business win, the businesspeople can understand what it means to them.

The inverse of the lockout is the trap—which explains to the prospect exactly why the lockout does not matter and is actually a bad idea.

The Lockout Case Study

At Rational, a computer software company, we had a powerful lockout feature that we were able to use extremely successfully against our competitors. Regardless of the huge price difference between us and all the other alternatives, we were about justifying that higher price. Rational had a revolutionary capability to see the impact of a software change before you actually made the change, and once you determined that you wanted the change, you only needed to change the pieces of the software that changed rather than entire software application. This capability was called incremental compilation. Today, this capability may seem commonplace, but in the late '80s, this was both unique and powerful feature.

This lockout was the key capability that we used because no one was even within years of having this feature. We were ruthless in building up the benefits of this capability by both showing the technical teams within the prospective accounts and building simple ROI calculators to show that each change would cost thousands of dollars and weeks of delay of delivery of new releases for the software applications.

The beauty of this lockout is that it has both a technical side and a business side, and as long as the salespersons were able to communicate both sides, they were able to win the deal. The most successful salespeople were able connect the experiential pain to not having incremental compilation. For the technical decision makers, it would make their lives simpler because they did not have to wait, sometimes for hours, to make changes. For the business players, the experience is how they felt about missing deadlines and the impact on their career.

After years of winning huge deals away from all our competitors, they scrambled to come up with weak imitations of this functionality, but it was too little and too late, and we were able to gain market share like a steamroller.

The trap. Even in a new market, the competitive landscape becomes defined quickly, and each competitor establishes its lockouts and knows its competitors' lockouts. The inverse of a lockout is a trap, which is either set for you to step into or left for you to set. If your competitor has been into an account before you and you know it, then you will need to make sure you do not step into the traps he has no doubt set (assuming he is a shrewd competitor). If you are the first one into an account, you will want to set a trap for your competitor.

For example: Standards are a typical lockout/trap item. There will be standards that you have and your competitor does not and vice versa. If you are asked very early in the call if you support a particular standard, then you know a trap has been set for you. Do not spring it. The best way to avoid a trap is to address the issue before it is asked so that you have the opportunity to explain your position without being defensive and save the prospect the embarrassment of having to ask the question.

What will your competitor do once they sense that they are not the favorite?

An example of a trap:

"Industry standards" is the most common trap that competitors set. It is a simple trap to set and can take hours to get out of. In the database, one of the standards that defined the use of databases was Structured Query Language or SQL. If the competitor supported the language, then they would make it the most important requirement. In the early '90s, the race to support the SQL standard was on, and it was the trap that the vendors who supported it used. The companies did not yet support it would get stuck in the trap, and few could get out of.

The end run. The end run is the strategy to go around the technical recommendation and straight to the business owner of the problem and explain why the criteria and rules were wrong. The unstated message is "If you do not go with my product rather than the one you are considering, the future of your company is in grave danger." It is an attempt to leverage the purse strings to force the technicians to reevaluate. There are a few proactive measures that can be taken to prevent the end run. First, prepare your contacts for the possibility that competitors will be bitter and may try something untoward to influence the proceedings. Second, lead your contacts to explain to the competitors that the evaluation phase has been put on hold and it may take a great deal longer to determine which product will be selected. Third, have your contacts express positive feedback to your competitors as a way for them to avoid unwanted phone calls.

The end run is the key reason that it is so important to start the business win as early in the sales process as possible. That way, if you need to do the end run, you will have established enough of a relationship that you'll be given the opportunity to be heard. If you win the technical recommendation, then you will have the opportunity to warn the business-win players what is in store for them from your competitors.

Neutral (or Undetermined)

You know you are in the neutral state of the technical win when you are getting questions, and you are receiving both positive and negative feedback. The good news is that you are getting news. In this position, you must follow the law of divide and concur because you will get the most accurate information from one-on-one interactions. And this communication preferably takes place off-site where you can learn about the rules and the power structure.

Dominate their time and establish deeper relationships on the business side so that you have a base from which you can recover if things go awry. The strategies that work best on the business side are twofold:

1. Provide reference calls and, better yet,
2. arrange a field trip to a customer who has implemented your product and would share why they purchased.

The business side needs to hear the business reasons and why these reasons are so important. They are not interested in any individual technical feature that the competitors may have planted.

The most dangerous thing about being in the undetermined state is that you are most likely not the favorite. And using the fundamental law—what is not overtly positive is covertly negative—well, draw your own conclusions.

Not the Favorite

How do you know that you are not the favorite? It's not as easy to determine as you may think because they are not going to tell you at first and maybe not at all. The signals will be that momentum is broken and calls go unreturned. You start to hear questions about the known competitor lockouts. The feature that was never a priority is now the most important requirement. This type of thing should set off the alert bells.

When you suspect that you are not the favorite, there are several possible responses—which can be used in any combination:

- Get with the most positive player you have and seek to discover what has changed and who is not on board.
- Get product management, even the VP of engineering, involved. They live the feature issue. Well managed, this will give the naysayer the opportunity to gain visibility and feel important by establishing a relationship with your company.
- Execute the end run.

When executing the end run:

- Don't ask permission from anyone to meet with the business owner.
- Bring in higher authority: the business owner will feel important and will be less likely to say no. (Bringing in the higher authority also gives you an out with the players you have a relationship with by simply blaming the higher authority.)
- Change the rules such that business issues trump technical issues.

Muddy the waters. If the end run fails, the approach is to reset the rules. The "muddy the waters" strategy is to reset the rules and introduce new alternatives. By muddying the waters, you buy time to unseat the current favorite. To counteract the "muddy the waters" strategy, be prepared and set traps for the alternatives. Reaffirm with your contacts why the rules are what they are. Warn the prospect about the possibility of a "muddy the waters" campaign being employed by your competitors and remind him that it would affect the process and jeopardize his ability to meet the deadline.

Finally, let's take a look at the players who are typically involved in determining a technical recommendation:

The end users. These are the people who will be using the product once it is purchased. There are typically just a few involved in the evaluation phase. They are challenging because each will have his own preferences that are often the opposite of everyone else's.

The naysayers. These are the people who just have to approve your product or service. They care only about their niche in the company and will not use the product. An example might be the security group or standards monitoring group.

The leader. This is the person who will make the final recommendation. He knows the issues inside out and will push you. The leader will delegate the work on evaluation to others who may try to expand the requirements far beyond what is really desired or needed.

Keeping the Momentum Going

With each key play, think ahead about three things that will keep the momentum going and be very concerned if momentum is broken. The momentum item needs to have a date when it must either happen, be cancelled, or be rescheduled. Some ideas for keeping the momentum going might include the following:

- Reference call
- Future product releases call
- Jointly developed presentation and demo
- Off-site coffee or meal
- Working together on an implementation plan

Building Your Map for Gaining the Technical Win

It is time to apply what you have learned to building your own map to the technical win. The first step is to identify the players who will be involved. The most important player is the technical leader, so think back to the deals that you have worked on and ask yourself who was typically the person needed to be convinced that your product was the right product. You also want to determine the roles of each of the players in the decision process.

Determining the milestones of the technical win is the next step, which will give you the direction you will need to go. Again, review past deals and talk over the deals that your colleagues have completed to determine what the flow has been. Milestones that we have typically seen are presentation, custom demonstration, pilot, group demonstration of pilot, and jointly built implementation plan. Having many milestones gives you options to share with your prospects, and the more reasons you have for them to spend time with you, the higher the probability that you will get the technical recommendation.

Once your map to the technical win is drawn, you will have a sense of where you are, what is going to happen next, and what needs to happen next.

Sample view of the technical win:

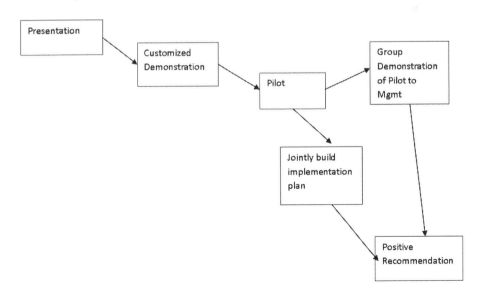

Chapter 8

THE BUSINESS WIN

The business win is having in hand the prospect's irreversible commitment to purchase, usually in the form of a purchase order or contract. The business win is best treated as a separate selling effort from the technical win because it is possible to lose the technical recommendation and still gain the business win. It is true that very experienced salespeople may ignore the technical win and focus only on the business win. And they can be very successful with this strategy, but they leave themselves open to getting hamstrung by a shrewd competitor who can team with the technical decision makers and capture the deal.

If the business win is not started as soon as the technical win, you will not have the relationships that will be needed in the case of losing the technical recommendation. Too often, the business win is not begun until the technical win is secured. This is far too late and leads to false deals and to deals that take longer and become smaller. The business campaign should begin at the same time as the technical campaign, and the two should run concurrently. It is harder to work the business campaign because the business players do not know why they are dealing with you, not yet having decided to select your product.

Quid pro quo is the most powerful technique and should be used as the method to gain introduction to the person who will sponsor you from a financial standpoint. The technical players will always want something, and at the first sizeable request, you should exchange an introduction to the business players for fulfilling their request. A relationship will need to be established with the sequence of people who will need to approve the purchase. In each case, that is, individually, they will need to understand why they might approve your offering over the alternatives.

The biggest mistake salespeople make in the business campaign—after not working the business win in parallel from the beginning—is not learning the language that the businesspeople talk. Businesspeople focus on the operations, execution, and leadership issues. They care about revenue, expenses, and the competitiveness of the business. They want to know how this purchase will affect these areas of the business, how it will impact the bottom line. They do not care about your product's bells and whistle, no matter how cool. They do not want to see demonstrations (which take valuable time), but they do want to learn about your company's suitability as a partner. And they want to know what experiences other companies like their own have had when they have used your product.

The Business Players

The players in the business campaign are very diverse: they have very different motives and views. They do share a disinterest in products and features and a supreme interest in the business issues and outcomes your product will support, but that's probably about as far as the similarities between them go. Their interests are often political, almost always economic, and certainly financial.

The Sliding Forecast

Every sales manager knows the sliding forecast. The sliding forecast is what happens when deals on the forecast slide from month to month and quarter to quarter. The salesperson does not really grasp it because the prospect says nothing but great things about the product and how badly he needs it. The prospect meets with you and shares information openly, but still the deal is not closing. There is always just one more approval required, and then it will be done. But the deal never gets done, it never closes, and the salesperson never learns what he's doing wrong.

The preeminent cause of the sliding forecast is the failure to recognize the fact that every deal has two major components—the technical win *and* the business win—and the corollary (the failure to recognize that you cannot rely on a technical player to get the business win for several reasons). The technical player may not know how to help you win the business, and there's a good chance that he has no experience with the buying process in his own company. Moreover, the technical player does not want to lose the help and support that you've been giving, and he doesn't want it to end. The junior sales rep is also more comfortable talking with the technical players because they are more accessible and they have the product in common.

Salespeople tend to be optimistic. One of our salespeople said a deal was worth $1.7 million. I asked, out of curiosity, "Have you met the guy who's going to foot the bill?" "Well, no," came the timid reply. It turned out to be a $100,000 deal.

Remember the case of the mature-looking seventeen-year-old boy going into a Porsche dealership. He knows everything there is to know about Porsches. He knows just what he wants: year, make, model, color, and interior, even custom stereo system. The inexperienced salesman is all excited (of course unaware of the child's minority) and spends all afternoon with the boy. After several hours, he begins to draw up the paperwork. Just then the boy's father comes in and, a bit perturbed, says, "Son, we're already late for practice—get in the car."

The technical buyer, like the seventeen-year-old Porsche shopper, does not have financial decision-making authority. He cannot write the check. He must take you to the economic, or business, buyer. The business buyer, by contrast, is likely to take you to the technical buyer to see if your product actually works. He has political, financial, or user experience, but not technical experience.

The junior salesperson tends to focus on the product's functionality. He may be very successful in convincing the technical decision makers that they absolutely must have his product. But he is likely to fall flat when it comes to getting the business win because of several issues:

- First, the junior salesperson is naive enough to believe that getting the technical win is enough and that the technical players will naturally get the business win for him.
- Second, it is a rare salesperson who will be capable of speaking to all the issues of the different players that will be involved in any deal. The good news is that they will not have to. The strategy of pulling in their own executives to speak with their counterparts at the prospect organization is always wise. The business players need their issues addressed and their questions answered. When a junior rep talks to them about features and functions, the business player rolls his eyes and starts to think about his next meeting. Here, as with all player interactions, the first law comes into play: everyone will ultimately act in his own self-interest.
- Third, in many cases, the technical players do not want you to gain access to the business players. This is an area that you need to manage very carefully. It is a real and dangerous sign when the technical players are blocking you because it can mean that they have not yet briefed the business players regarding what they are doing, or most likely, they do not want to lose control over the decision. They also may see it as unnecessary and see no value in introducing you. So it is very important to build trust. But once they ask for something, it is time to request an introduction and possibly pull in a higher authority from your organization so that the business win can begin.

What Can Go Wrong in the Business Campaign?

The biggest mistake salespeople make in pursuit of the business win is failure to supply the key business player with a compelling enough reason to meet. The business players need to have a strong reason to meet with you, especially early in the process, lest they view you as just another salesperson looking to rush a decision and end-run the technical due diligence. The business player's natural tendency is to buy as little as possible, which is, of course, the opposite of what the seller wants.

What differentiates the Maverick method from the other selling methods?

- Miller Heiman's Strategic Selling® identifies the economic buyer but has no strategy to get the actual business decision nor what to do if you do not get the technical or business win.
- Holden's Power Base Selling® focuses only on the fox and getting to the fox and does not take into account how to close the deal if there is no fox or champion.

The Maverick method dissects the sale into the major parts that need to be worked on both in parallel and in sequence. The Maverick method shows how to get the business win and what to do when things go wrong. We tell you what the business players want to hear about and several strategies that work. And we provide insight into what your competitors will be doing to derail you.

The Business Players

- The business unit managers who own the problem that your product is solving: They typically will not have the spending approval for the total amount needed, so they are not the final economic decision makers. Their creditability is critical because, without it, you will be on your own to convince the final decision maker.
- Everyone above the business unit manager up to the final signature on the purchase request: How high you go in the organization will depend largely on the amount of money that you are seeking. Typically, anything above fifty thousand dollars will require a vice president to sign, and anything over one hundred thousand dollars will require the president to sign. Often, when a purchase exceeds a million dollars, it will require the board of directors. The approval of the purchase will depend on the size of the organization and how long it has been in business. Your business player most likely will not know this process or the timing of it, so it is up to the salesperson to determine.
- Any necessary legal approval that will depend on the contractual requirements that your company and the

prospect's company require: This process can be simply an administrative process and just take time, or this can be a real-deal killer. This process needs to be managed to make sure that all your work is not wasted. Any deal killers that come up in the legal phase should be talked about from the beginning of the sale to determine whether they can be overcome.

- All necessary purchase approval, like the legal approval process or the purchasing group process: The purchasing group will want to add value to their company by trying to get additional discount. It is very important that you have support from a power player for the prospect so that, when you speak to the purchasing representative, you can explain that the discount has already been pushed to the greatest it can be.

The Natural Sales Laws That Apply to the Business Campaign

- **Nothing happens unless you make it happen.** The business win will not happen without someone driving it. Certainly, the internal technical recommendation will help start the business win, but someone needs to explain the business value and write up the justification. If the salesperson leaves it to his or her internal sponsor to do the business win, the risk is increased and control is reduced. If the salesperson drives the business win, he or she controls the process and can direct it in his or her favor. By providing a draft business justification with the formal technical recommendation, you have the framework to build a formal justification that can function as a mutual project to work on.
- **Everyone will ultimately act in his own self-interest.** Knowing that everyone will do what serves them best will do two things for you: First, you will know what they are interested in, and second, it will explain what they will ultimately do. The Maverick seller will test the words that each player uses versus the actions that they take. Everyone knows that it is the player's actions that matter, but we often get distracted by the words that they say. When you constantly review the actions that the player takes, you will get a better sense as to what their words

really mean. Our judgment can also be clouded by our own best interest: our need to close the deal is our interest but not our prospect's. We need to remember and concentrate on what is in the prospect's best interest and sell to it.

- **What is not overtly positive is covertly negative.** At the business win, if you are not getting consistent cooperation and feedback, then you need to recognize that something is wrong, and you need to correct it. When you have a technical win, there will be a need to continue with the momentum because the natural reaction after the technical win is for the prospect to ask whether this product make business sense for them.
- **It is not the product.** The product is the focus of the technical win, but for the business win, it is all about the impact the product will have on the business. The topics that the business players care about are financial and political, not functional.

What to do if you do not get the business win: Regardless of the success with the technical team and the business owner of the problem, getting money from any organization is always a challenge. The proposal can make great business sense and have a short return on investment, but you always need to be prepared for rejection or delay. The fallback or plan B should be prepared so that momentum is not completely lost; your plan B should, at a minimum, commit the prospect to your company's product. By committing the prospect to your product, you will have them as a customer and will have the opportunity to continue the selling process. If the prospect does not make any financial commitment to your product and just says that they need more time, this will greatly reduce the likelihood that anything will happen.

The Business Justification

The most powerful tool to capture the business win is the business justification. This is a document that is developed jointly with the prospect. Having a draft of a business justification that you can customize to each particular prospect is very important. Technical players will have to prepare some kind of a report on their due diligence, so if you can give them a framework, you are solving two problems at once. First, you are helping the prospect get his work done. But second, and more important, you are framing the justification on your strengths. By working on the justification jointly with the prospects, you are getting a lot of face time—or at least e-mail communication—which will give you greater insight into how the organization works and how to develop your strategy. And because the technical players are unlikely to know how to build a business justification, they will need a great deal of help.

The business player will typically be required to write something up as well, and your draft business justification is a great fit for this need. You can find on the Internet templates for a business justification that will help you structure a successful document that can be presented to senior management and board members, justifying the need for a purchase:

The Business Justification Outline

i. Executive summary
    1. Outline the history of why the technical evaluation was done and what business problems it will solve. The executive summary should be only a couple of paragraphs and should be targeted at the final business player that you require approval from.
    2. The proposed solution: Describe at a high level the recommended solution that focuses on solving the business problem and not just the product.

ii. Requirements
    1. Talk to the business issues that are problems today and are costing the business. The costs need to be outlined and described; they can be current costs or future costs.

ii. Alternatives
    1. Discuss the competitors that were evaluated and why they did not meet the decision criteria. It is very important that a detailed and fair evaluation was completed and your product was the only viable solution. This part is best if you write it so as to have the most detailed description of the alternatives and then let the prospect review it.

    2. It is important to lock out everyone else completely so that the door is closed behind your solution.

iv. Evaluation process

    1. Talk to the process that was used for evaluation; it is key to explaining the depth to which they went to make the selection.

    2. Make sure every possible question is answered and every issue is raised.

    3. Develop a table of requirements and have your product as the only one that meets all the requirements.

    4. Include reference calls that have validated that your product has been used in the same type of situation.

    v. Recommendation: Describe in detail the recommended approach that maps business requirements with product and implementation issues.

vi. ROI

    1. The most important part is the ROI because the ROI justifies the money that is being exchanged for the product. If the ROI is done well, the prospect will view the product as an investment versus and expense.

    2. The business players want to know what they are getting for their money and how long it is going take to get their investment back. The ROI should be worked on jointly and project a payback in less than one year. The ROI should include both cost reductions and revenue increases.

vii. Implementation plan

    1. You want to show that you have thought through the issues beyond just the purchase and have a well-thought-out plan to implement the solution.

    2. You need to balance showing what it takes to make the product successful against the cost of making the product successful.

viii. Schedule

    1. The schedule sets the deadline for getting to the fulfillment of the vision and is the date that the prospect cares about.

2. Provide a date for each step and an owner; working backward will drive each needed decision. These dates will create and maintain the momentum; the timeline will bring awareness, which will cause the need to take action.
3. The date that you care most about is of course the purchase order, which will define the achievement of the business win.

Sample Map to the Business Win:

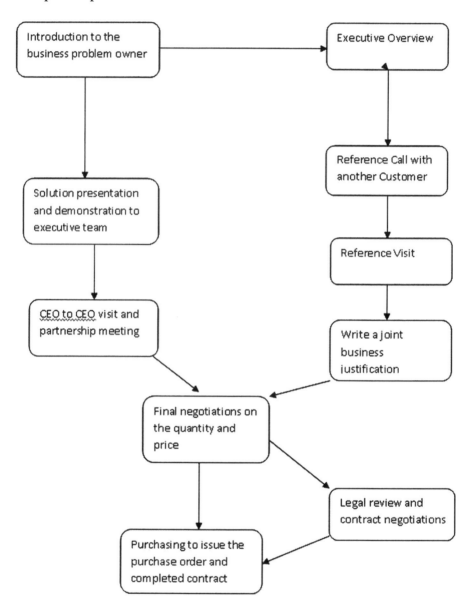

Chapter 9

MAVERICK STRATEGIES

*In preparing for battle I have always found that plans are
useless, but planning is indispensable.*
—Dwight D. Eisenhower

William E. Rothschild asked, "What do you want to achieve or
avoid? The answers to this question are objectives. How will you go
about achieving your desired results? The answer to this you can
call strategy." That is the sense in which we are discussing strategy.
Strategies are skillful maneuvers for successfully executing the
selling process. This is an area on which few sellers focus enough
attention. Salespeople are typically looking for the magic words that
will make the sale, that will make up for a lack of characteristics,
skills, or a strategy. There are no magic words. It takes knowledge,
practice, and discipline. But the good news is we have found that the
smarter and more consistent approach is to take what you already
do best and apply it to the selling process. That is, your unique
talents, properly applied, can work.

When people try to learn new selling skills, they often become
overwhelmed and end up sounding phony and incongruent.
We have found that the most effective approach, the Maverick

approach, is to figure out what you do best, the skills that come naturally to you, and base your strategy on those skills. You must, of course, master the *process* in which the strategy plays. If you do want to expand your repertoire, to add more arrows to the proverbial quiver, then practice just one skill at a time until you master it.

Some Basic Strategies

Relationship building. Relationship building is the most common selling strategy and the most recognized skill of talented salespeople. Of course, if relationship building was enough for successful sales, there would be a lot more killer salespeople. But this is strategy without a complete understanding and command of the process. It is often said that people buy from people they like or, more to the point, from people they trust. It is true that people will do more for people they like and enjoy spending time with, but if a competitor knows the *process* (i.e., how to position his or her product and lock yours out), the players could be your best friends, but they will not buy from you. Relationship building is only an effective strategy in the context of process.

Steve was the master of the relationship-building strategy and very successful as a salesperson. He was a very nice guy and a pleasure to speak with—really a joy to be around—but he knew that people didn't buy from him because of his personality. Steve was aware that it was his skill at relationship building that gave him insight into organizational needs and how clients felt they could best solve these needs. He would have breakfast with one of the several guides he had befriended in an account to catch up on what had happened since the last client meeting and to help his guide with any issues he may be facing, reassuring his guide that he was there as backup.

Steve was difficult to manage: He was never in the office and was always late with his forecast and expenses. But he was always welcome to all of his prospects and customers. He understood intuitively that because no one bought from him at his office, he needed to be out there in the field building relationships. He realized that if he was not connecting with each key player in a prospect organization, then his competitor would be.

Steve was bold—which is not to say brazen. He would make dinner plans with the CEO of each of his prospects for the purpose of getting them away from the office and learning what really makes them tick. He was very careful never to use these opportunities for a sales pitch but rather to gain insight into what these CEOs cared about, what they were focused on, what kept them up at night. Steve's colleagues accused him of hobnobbing, relying on his charm and his expense account to close deals. But the truth is that Steve had mastered the strategy of relationship building. He had discovered the secret of reading people correctly, knowing when they were being straight with him and when they were brushing him off. Steve mastered the *relationship-building* strategy and leveraged it to become a Maverick.

Product passion. Another common strategy is to be passionate about your product and enthusiastic when presenting it. Enthusiasm is very contagious. This strategy will certainly help you with the technical players and is very powerful in gaining the technical win—but it won't work with the business players. Business players are looking for business results and outcomes. While they may appreciate your passion and enthusiasm, they will not be swayed by it.

Product passion and enthusiasm tend to be the domain of end users and their ilk. These are rare traits among typical salespeople, but they can make for powerful strategy. Henry was an engineer-turned-salesperson. He brought to sales a very unusual mixture of deep technical knowledge and skill and an ability to see and describe the unique value of a product in relation to business outcomes. His transition from engineering management to sales was born from frustration with the sales organizations' apparent inability to communicate product differentiators to prospective clients. He had held the profession of selling in somewhat low esteem based on a general sense that salespeople are overpaid and underskilled. Now he was one of them and determined to show himself better than the rest. Henry was a master at the presentation and demonstration, but at first he was unable to connect with a customer's pain or see what might drive that customer to the next stage. He was brilliant with the technical win because he could always wow the end users, but it took some time to learn that each buyer in an organization has his own language and really cares about the product only to the extent that it adds value to his role within the company.

Then Henry teamed up with a manager who taught him to distinguish between the technical win and the business win, and the rest is history. Henry's passion and enthusiasm covered a multitude of sins while he learned the skills that make for great sales. His drive and intellect also helped to make up for the foibles. Now his passion and enthusiasm remain unabated, but they are under rein and used strategically.

Account entry point: two strategies. There are typically two ways to approach and enter an account. ***Bottom Up***: This strategy is used when the salesperson initially approaches the end users of the product, the people who are experiencing the pain or might see a need for your innovative or disruptive technology. Here, you gain the technical win first and then work your way up to the decision makers. ***Top Down***: This strategy is to enter the account at the business player or senior executive level with a strong business case for the use of your product and then use executive support to work with the technical players.

We have found that both of these strategies work and that neither is necessarily preferable. Some Mavericks use one; some use the other. It is really a matter of personal preference and comfort level. You should use whichever you're most comfortable with. The thing that separates the Maverick from the B Player is that the Maverick actually uses one or the other as a strategic maneuver; he does not just work with prospects that come to him through the leads produced by marketing.

Advanced Maverick Strategies

Mavericks have developed several advanced strategies that are teachable and repeatable. Anyone can learn them and put them into practice. They are not difficult to master, but they may require some internal selling. Most companies are not predisposed to handle these strategies for their salespeople, but we've never worked with a company that wasn't willing to at least listen to new ideas regarding selling. Indeed, every company wants to be successful, and most are crying out for leadership in how to close more deals.

"We're all in this together." This is a very powerful strategy that works particularly well with very large deals. It is most applicable to the new product / new market sell. This strategy brings to bear the full resources of the selling company. Of course, this strategy does not scale to all the salespeople of even a midsized firm, but for one or two Maverick salespeople, it can be incredibly useful. This strategy is the best and highest use of the divide-and-concur law as applied to internal as well as external forces. It involves matching the players in your own company with their counterparts in the prospect company. For example, arrange for your VP of engineering to meet with the prospect's VP of engineering. The power of this strategy is twofold. First, it is an excellent example of how to keep the momentum going. Second, it gives the prospect a comfort level and a sense that he is important. This strategy reduces risk.

Karen is a Maverick. She is not a master of product knowledge nor particularly interested in the details. Her colleagues tease her about never having gone on a sales call alone. But this is not in fact a weakness; rather, it is her great strength and talent. For Karen is a master of the *"we're all in this together"* strategy of sales. Karen has built enormous trust internally—with her colleagues, her managers, and even her CEO. They trust her and are eager to support her because she only brings them in strategically—where they can bring value—never as cannon fodder. She always seems to know precisely who would bring the most value to a client meeting—and inevitably shows up with that person: always the right person at the right time. She knows her own strengths and her weaknesses and augments them with key players. She would describe her style as a deal manager rather than being a lone wolf.

Again, it is always strategic. It is never reactionary or responding to a crisis. Karen doesn't just bring people along for the sake of companionship or backup. Karen always has a plan for how a colleague can contribute positively to the progression of the sale. Karen can do the work of three salespeople because there are always others working with her clients on her behalf. And by leveraging even her CEO, she is able to get meetings others would never dream of arranging.

The *"we're all in this together"* strategy requires a great deal of coordination and preparation and is dependent on the interpersonal skills of the people that you bring into the account. There is nothing worse than bringing in an executive who does not have solid communication skills or team-building skills or an executive who appears to care more for his own success than the success of the prospect. So the first question you have to ask yourself is "Who are the players that bring value to the Maverick team? Who will benefit the relationship, exuding the right impression, rather than be a detriment?" Who doesn't have war stories of bringing in a manager or an executive who steps in it or puts his foot in his mouth, causing weeks of repair work to get the process back on track? So before finalizing the team, poll your colleagues and find out how potential team members have done in the past in front of prospects. You must set the team up for success.

As a Maverick, you want to control the process from beginning to end. Set the agendas for the meetings, guide your executive in what to do and what to say and, more importantly, in what not to do and what not to say. Here's an example of what can happen if you don't prepare for every contingency within the realm of the possible: Some years ago, I took a customer out for a fancy steak dinner and made the mistake of inviting my unprepared and unrehearsed manager. As we were bonding over cocktails, the customer was explaining how his company was building its future strategy on one of our products. My manager chose this moment to point out that, in fact, we were cancelling that product from our suite of offerings. Well, imagine how that went over. I quickly explained that, while true, we had a replacement strategy and would continue to support the product well into the future. But my manager kept on down the path of how our company was going a different direction. He just wouldn't stop. It was a train wreck. I kicked him under the table, but he just didn't get that this was not the time or the place to drop bad news. This was the time and place to take the opportunity to learn more about what our customer was looking to do and figure out how we might partner together for mutual benefit. I take full credit for the gaff: I should have prepared the manager in advance—suggesting that there might be a more appropriate time to share the news about our evolving product strategy. But really, who could have imagined that an otherwise experienced sales manager would be so crass as to say something so negative over cocktails?

"Refuse to lose." This strategy is, precisely as it sounds, refusal to allow a loss. It requires excellent interpersonal skills that will allow you access to the players who have already decided not to move forward with you. Obviously, even Mavericks lose sometimes—even the best lose deals—but the best never give up. You can do everything right, but people are people. They are unpredictable. And there are always new and unexpected players and competitors. The Maverick treats it all as opportunity.

Now it may seem to be more of an attitude than a strategy; it is both. It is certainly the most consistent belief system that we have noticed among the Mavericks we've studied. Refusing to lose keeps the focus on the end goal every day and keeps the salesperson focused on the fact that it is his or her responsibility to win. The characteristics that define the "refuse to lose" strategy/attitude are determination, persistence, and the belief that each deal is winnable.

A powerful example of the *"refuse to lose"* mentality comes from outside the sales arena and touches the hearts and minds of any who remembers it. On September 11, 2001, United Flight 93 was highjacked. It was the intention of the highjackers to crash the plane into the Unites States Capitol or possibly the White House. The Twin Towers and the Pentagon had already been attacked on that fateful morning. An Oracle salesperson, Todd Beamer, and several other Maverick passengers had learned what was happening from their loved ones via cell phone calls. That day, they stepped out of their roles as ordinary airline passengers and into the roles of heroes. They refused to lose. Winning meant not allowing the highjackers to win. They decided that dying passively and doing what they were told to do were not acceptable; it was simply not going to happen. They banded together, risking their safety and possible death, to recapture the aircraft from the terrorists. They chose to refuse to lose, to win control over their destiny. They fought for their lives, took the control away from the terrorists, and changed the course of history. They did not allow the highjackers to complete their mission. They could have sat back in fare and let things take their course—but not on their watch. They rose up taking control of their destiny and refused to lose. This is Maverick thinking at its best.

This strategy must be used throughout the process, not only once it becomes apparent that you are not going to win a deal. The sooner you sense that you may not be winning, the sooner you can adjust your strategy. Remember the law: "Whatever is not overtly positive is covertly negative." The B Player will walk away the moment he discovers he has lost the deal; he will turn his attention to other opportunities. The Maverick will not give up so easily. He will work with his guides in the account to understand what's happening, who's behind the selection, and what rules they are applying to justify the decision. He'll then determine whether the player who is pushing for the competitive product can be converted in order to decide whether to use a direct or indirect strategy.

There are those who believe that once you've lost a deal, any continuation is throwing good time after bad. But those who can execute this strategy often are able to regain quickly deals that others would pass by.

So what exactly is the "refuse to lose" strategy, and how do you execute it? It takes iron will and great confidence but also finesse to break down the lockout that has been put in place without appearing rude or unconscionable. It can be done in any number of ways, from the end run to the sharp price cut. The point is that you simply refuse to lose, and by persisting, you win the deal.

"The kingpin strategy." We have alluded to this strategy in earlier chapters, but this strategy is so powerful that it deserves a deeper explanation. The kingpin strategy, when executed well, makes selling so much easier. The strategy is to identify the kingpin within a territory and then do whatever it takes to win that account. Then use the kingpin reference and case study to win the next tier of accounts. When leaders move in a direction, others follow. There is nothing more convincing than a rave review from a market leader. This strategy requires an experienced salesperson to be able to build the connection with the kingpin—which is likely a difficult account to penetrate. More junior salespeople will focus on the low-hanging fruit instead. The problem with low-hanging fruit is that each deal is tactical and independent. Without the kingpin strategy, you are not really building a business.

Kent was the talented salesperson who taught us the "kingpin strategy." He was very creative and very meticulous: he never made a move without first working out a strategy. Kent had been selling to the federal government for about ten years when we met him. He was a real student of government organization and the interdependencies of the different agencies. He made it his business to know the lay of the land so well that when he figured out whom the kingpin was and made the sale, the rest of the agencies would fall in line like dominoes. His whole approach, in fact, was based on the domino principle, and so his strategy was developed with the endgame (falling dominoes) in mind. He developed his presentations to describe what the world would look like when the entire government was standardized on his product. He leveraged every evaluation—and even every positive meeting—to move closer and closer to the kingpin. When he finally arrived in the kingpin's office, after only a year, he was able to capture the entire federal government in one fell swoop. It actually forced his own company to change its business model in order to meet the needs of his army of new customers.

The mistake that some people make with this strategy is working only on the kingpin—and no one else—until the kingpin is won over. The great thing is to work all the angles and leverage every available resource. The Maverick understands that the kingpin will take time and patience. Work on those near the kingpin as you formulate the strategy and line up the dominoes. But always keep your eye on the prize. Kent was a Maverick par excellence—he used every opportunity to build a groundswell of interest and support so that, when the kingpin finally made the purchase, all the pieces fell into place.

"It all comes down to one thing." This strategy is about finding the one reason that a prospect *needs* to purchase your product now. This was a common strategy with the Mavericks we studied. It may seem simple, but it can be challenging to determine what the one thing actually is and how best to position it. The power in the "one thing" strategy is that all the players will have a clear understanding of why they are purchasing the product. Typically, the "one thing" is a lockout feature of the product that matches to a financial benefit. The "one thing" can be technical for the technical users

and financial for the business players—they don't all have to be sold on the same thing. The key is to find that single reason that will sway each player and link it to the end result.

At Rational, we had the ultimate "one thing" feature, and it gave us market supremacy. It was a functionality that worked as a lockout almost invariably and allowed us to be extremely successful against our competitors despite the enormous price difference between us and every other alternative. Rational had developed the revolutionary capability to see the impact of a software change without actually having to make the change. That is to say, it allowed you to see what was going to happen with each change you made to the system and, therefore, allowed you to pinpoint those changes that had merit. It then allowed you to make specific, targeted changes without changing the entire software application. Today, this capability is commonplace, but at the time, in the late 1980s, it was a unique and game-changing feature.

We hammered this "one thing" lockout capability relentlessly because no one else was within years of having this capability. We would wow the technical teams in prospective accounts and build simple ROI calculators that showed how each change by a competitor would cost thousands of dollars and weeks of delay on the delivery of new releases of software applications. It appealed to both the technical end users and the business buyers, allowing savvy salespeople to communicate with both sides and win the deal. After years of winning huge deals away from all of our competitors, they scrambled and came up with weak imitations, but it was too little, too late. We gained market share like a juggernaut, all based on the strategy that it all comes down to one thing.

"Let's be partners." This strategy is most powerful when coupled with the kingpin strategy and the "we're all in this together" strategy because the only thing better than winning the kingpin account is joining the kingpin as a partner. Partnerships are desirable on any number of levels. The customer will have the product direction in their favor so that new features are available to them first. Moreover, the customer will want to ensure the success of the product so that their investment is protected. The value to the seller is in both the

obvious financial reward and, from a marketing standpoint, the partnerships bringing tremendous credibility.

Mike had a slightly different approach that leveraged both the relationship strategy and the "we're all in this together" strategy to create a strategy uniquely his own. He would, in essence, "marry" the customer to his own company. He would get product development at his own company involved so that his customers' requirements would make it into the next version of the product—and any problems with the product would be fixed in a timely fashion. Mike's marketing team would work with his customers' marketing teams to create success stories and joint advertising. Mike was able to lock out the competition by making his customers feel like family. Why would they possibly look elsewhere to have problems solved? He would even have the CEOs of all his customers visit his own corporate headquarters to meet everyone and get a sense of the future direction of the company. As it happens, Mike was able to get three times the revenue from his customers than any other salesperson.

As the partnership broadens and deepens, it will bond the two organizations. A partnership is the formalization of the quid pro quo law without the ping-pong nature of quid pro quo on each item. The typical mistake in the partnership strategy is not formalizing it and then not executing it. The partnership should include sales, product development, support, and marketing, not just sales. When properly executed, the partnership strategy might include joint ad campaigns, site visits with key prospects, product feedback, and enterprise-size purchasing.

"I'm in control." It's true that it's hard to control other people, but it is possible to control the process. The first step to controlling the process is understanding the process. Without control of the process, you are simply reacting to the prospect, and those reactions are just too late to win the deal. You may feel that prospects do not want to be controlled—and you would be correct—but what they do want is to be led. They want to be led because they are on new ground and do not know how to purchase your product. They also most likely do not understand what needs to be done to complete the administration process of purchasing. This is why controlling

the process is so critical. The how-to is not hard, but it is not really explained or taught by sales training courses. The courses that we have studied focus only on the one-on-one, single call and explain that the larger complex sale is just a collection of small simple sales. This is just the tip of the iceberg. Without understanding the process and without having a strategy, you are on a treasure hunt without a treasure map. You are not in control.

There is a major difference between the A and B Players, and it is simple to tell the difference. First you can ask, "When is your next meeting with the prospect?" The B Player will say, "I have a call in to the prospect and should hear back soon." The A Player will give you the date, time, and place. Not getting a commitment to the next communication is a negative signal that there may be some covertly negative item that is not being shared. You need to dig deeper. The only legitimate reason for no specified future communication is that you did not propose a good enough reason for the prospect to meet or join a conference call.

The other part of control is momentum: the deal in motion tends to stay in motion, and a deal at rest tends to stay at rest. Without momentum, you do not have control because you will spend all your time trying to create momentum. Other than always arranging the next communication, momentum can be achieved by the divide-and-concur law. When you keep everyone focused on the deadline to receive the benefit of the product and then list all the items that need to take place, it will create that sense of urgency. Watching for any signal that momentum is slowing is vital. Once you sense slowed momentum, immediate action is required because there are two reasons why for a change: either the customer has a higher priority or they are moving forward with another product. Neither of the other reasons is going to help you, and you need to understand quickly what the cause is and come up with a strategy to get momentum back.

"The ecosystem." This strategy is very powerful because, although complex, it is repeatable. In every market, there is an ecosystem that includes product companies, service companies, and recruiting companies. Within this ecosystem, the Maverick salesperson leverages everyone else who is working within a prospective market.

He uses the natural interrelationships and interactions with the environment to bring the full extent of the system's resources to bear on his prospective client.

Our friend Ed was the master of the ecosystem strategy. He never did cold calls, and he never begged for a first call. Instead, he would build a network of all the product companies within a sector (his target market) and would then partner with the leading consulting companies that were targeting the market—and anyone else who he felt might be able to add value to the selling process, for that matter.

After having won several deals, Ed noticed that his customers were always looking for design tools just before they evaluated his product, so Ed met up with the leading design tool vendors in his territory and explained the value he could provide them. Ed would point out that he would share leads and would give endorsements to accounts that they were both working on. This partnering with other salespeople gave Ed more opportunities than he could handle.

Ed also met with the leading consulting companies that would implement not only his product, but also several others. Ed would determine the best and most professional people and then explain that he could also provide tremendous value by getting them work, asking only for an indirect reference in return. When Ed would meet with prospects, he would bring a complete solution to the table. Prospects inevitably felt that Ed understood their situation infinitely better than any of the other vendors. He was able to bring additional resources to the opportunity that solved problems that the prospect had—and not just the problem that his own product solved.

Part of the informal arrangement with the network of people and companies was that they would not share information with competitors and would not work with any of the other competitors. This is the risk inherent in the ecosystems strategy. These partnership relationships are not at the company level but at the personal, one-on-one basis. Trust is the key ingredient. It must be explained and committed to—with the knowledge that if the trust is broken, the arrangement will be ended. Ed would work with people who would also work with his competitors, but he was aware that whatever he said would most likely be shared with his competitors. He would rank his network of partners and would work it in the order of value.

Another of his tactics was to work with recruiters to move people who would not help him. The recruiter would call the accounts and competitors to get situational information and get them to interview with other opportunities. The recruiters would also help his prospects get the best people available. When Ed would be blocked and could not find any way around a particular person in the account, he would get his recruiter partners to pull that person out of his way. Ed was also great at managing the partners to make sure they did not know each other or how Ed was gaining such insight into the market and account knowledge.

"Baby steps." Island Exchange was a completely high-tech exchange that traded energy and other commodities all over the world—and all online. They were disgruntled with a current software vendor that they had built their exchange on because now that they were growing, they felt that the vendor was taking advantage of them. The vendor knew that it would be expensive to replace its product with any other, so it was not at all flexible on the licensing and pricing.

Enter Jean Claude who sold a competitive software product that was priced aggressively but was not yet as mature nor was it robust. Jean Claude was the master of the baby steps strategy. He had worked for several start-ups and was a smart salesman who knew how to work against seemingly insurmountable odds. As with most of the leads that Jean Claude received, the one from Island Exchange was not valued very highly because the inside salesperson did not feel that the prospect was serious. It already had purchased a competitive product, and in this market, it was very hard to swap out products because substantial investments were made in learning and development.

Jean Claude knew better. He had done this at several companies before and knew that it is not only possible, but also a fun challenge to win a deal from a competitor. The first call was set, and of course, there were no key decision makers there, and the focus was on a broad set of issues that spanned both the technical and business issues. The engineers who were assigned to the meeting had no business power but spent their time wanting to know licensing costs and out-year support cost—giving Jean Claude the clear impression that they just wanted to use him in the negotiations with their current vendor. Jean Claude deflected any cost questions, explaining that there are lots of variables and that much more understanding of what they wanted to do it on and on what types of hardware was needed to give an accurate view of the costs. He also gave the blanket statement that his company never loses on cost as a way to deflect, giving a cost answer to people who had no budget authority.

At the close of the first call, the usual request for an evaluation copy was brought up. Jean Claude agreed, noting that all he needed was a quick introduction to the CIO (who was the final technical decision maker and whose name came up several times during the call) who had not attended. The engineers said that the CIO, Martin, was a very busy man and that he does not like to meet with vendors until his team has approved the product. Jean Claude smiled and said he understood and that he would just need five minutes of his time. He also said that his VP requires a meeting with the CIO as part of their process. The engineers reluctantly walked Jean Claude to the CIO's office. Jean Claude then explained how well the meeting went and that he would like to understand from the CIO why he is currently in the market to evaluate his product. Jean Claude worked in a lockout by explaining that his product was an implementation of the new JAVA standard and that their current supplier was not and would not be for years. Island Exchange had made the switch to the JAVA standard as a way of leveraging new technology and increasing the productivity of their software development team. The introduction went well, but there was still no clear signal other than that they wanted a proposal that the CIO could use as a negotiations tool against his current supplier.

On the way to the office, Jean Claude's manager called and wanted to know how the meeting had gone and, more importantly, whether they were serious about the idea of switching products. Jean Claude explained that he saw an opportunity in that he had a follow-up meeting on Friday that week to begin the evaluation process. It was a stretch, but he knew that if he told his boss how hard it would be, his boss would have pulled the plug and asked Jean Claude to work on some other opportunity.

Friday that week, Jean Claude did not bring his product but wanted to understand their current use of the existing product. This frustrated them because they simply wanted to install it and say that they had done their due diligence, but Jean Claude knew he wanted to drag this out (i.e., baby step it as a way of building interest and gaining a deep understanding of how they were solving the current problem). By his not bringing the product, there was another quid pro quo that was available to Jean Claude at the end of the meeting. If he had brought the product, then it may have been his last meeting with them. The original meeting was set for an hour, but Jean Claude kept pulling in more and more players and, at the end, suggested that they go to dinner to talk over the process and get a stronger feel for whether Jean Claude might have a better solution. Jean Claude was able to pull out of their usage of the other product problems that they saw and issues that his product could solve. He knew that he would have to change the rules so that he could gain an advantage beyond price.

Jean Claude was able to build relationships with several of the engineers without threatening the powerbase. He gathered enough information to build up a concept of substantial pain with their current solution and evoked two lockout features that Island Exchange bought into. Unfortunately, he ran into several major technical issues with most of the product and its performance. The situation was shaky at best and was like a roller coaster over several months. After one particularly knotty meeting between Jean Claude's president and the CIO, the president remarked on the way back to the airport that he was wasting his time because the prospects hated them. Jean Claude, however, knew that if they were wasting their time, Island Exchange would have kicked them out by now. Thus, they continued their work with the product. Within a month, it was the end of Jean Claude's quarter, and he needed a deal to make his number, so he met with the CIO who held the IT budget and presented the business justification for the switch to his product. After several heated negotiations and many sleepless nights, a purchase was approved. Jean Claude's president was amazed—certain as he was that Jean Claude was pouring good money after bad. But Jean Claude knew what he was doing, and he knew how to take what everyone else thought was impossible and makes it possible.

Jean Claude shared with us that the easiest way to keep a deal alive and moving forward is to keep taking small steps forward, or baby steps. These steps are so nonthreatening that no one can really object to them, but before they know it, they have come to the conclusion that your product has great value and you are a trusted member of their team. Larger steps require larger decisions. By breaking the decision into smaller decisions, risk for everyone is lowered. From a selling standpoint, this is the simplest strategy to learn and apply because there is not much technique to it other than asking for the next step and knowing what type of step can be taken without scaring anyone off. The "baby steps" strategy is often confused with relationship selling, which is building a relationship with the client and hoping that, when the client needs his product, he will purchase it. The "baby steps" strategy is based on understanding how organizations purchase but knowing that the situation is so difficult that it will require much more background work and new ways to position the product.

These are not the only possible strategies but just a small sample. Each salesperson should build his or her own unique approach based on his or her own skill set, ask for feedback on what areas need to be worked on, and pick one skill a month to work on.

Chapter 10

THE MAVERICK MATRIX

The Maverick matrix is an array of the characteristics, skills, and attitudes that salespeople either have or need to develop. We have separated these skills into groups and put them in the order that they should be understood and developed.

Characteristics	C Player	B Player	A Player	Maverick
Proactive	Follower	Takes responsibility	Knows what to do and does it	Leads both the team and prospect
Intelligent	Is not intelligent or does not apply it	Understands what needs to be done	Knows the product and the market	Applies his intelligence to win and outsmart the competitors
Motivated	Does as little as needed to get by	Wants to be in the top 20%	Wants to be in the top 10%	Wants to be the best
Competitive	Feels prospects will do what they want	Likes to win but does not take it personally when they lose	Very Competitive and needs to win	Extremely competitive and winning is the only thing
Creative	Just does what he or she is told	Following the company process	Creates new ways to close the deal	Determined to find a way to win every deal

What's in it for me?

The beauty of a matrix like this is that it provides a basis for comparison and differentiation, both against the standard and against others—some of whom may be substantially more successful and, therefore, worthy of emulation. People are notoriously bad at self-analysis and can rarely pinpoint those attitudes and behaviors that actually make them more or less successful as compared to those behaviors that they *believe* make them successful. The skills shown here in the matrix are those that make people increasingly more successful. Mastery of them all makes one a Maverick. The matrix gives you a sense of what each level of player does differently and what separate them.

To determine what attitudes each players has about the major components or elements of selling, use the matrix as a guide. Learn the basics first and master them. The payoff will be immediate and considerable. The biggest mistake made by salespeople who are stuck in the land of the B Player is thinking that they already know the best way to sell and are already doing it. They don't, and they're not.

Look for a moment at the chart below that shows the attitudes of the different levels of players. Make an honest assessment and decide where you fall—and then decide whether selling is really your passion. There is nothing worse than being in the wrong job.

Attitudes	C Player	B Player	A Player	Maverick
Money	Pay the bills	Make target income	Leverage accelerators	Make the most in the company
Competition	You win some; you lose some	Knows how to work around them	Hates to lose and fights for every win	Marginalizes the competition, refusing to lose
Product	Depends on the product to sell	Knows how to position the product	Understands that it is the end result of what the product brings	Focuses on the end result of the business result the product brings
Territory	Territory makes the man	Depends on the quality of leads	Prospects without leads	Self-reliant and is successful regardless of the territory
Emotional Attachment	Detaches himself from the results	Takes some responsibility	Owns the result	Takes total responsibility for winning and losing
Work	Work to live and not live to work	Career oriented	Passionate about what they do	Selling is their profession and art form
Learning	As needed	Know it all	Hungry to learn more	Passion for learning every possible distinction
Motivation	Keeping their job	Making quota	Being in the top 10%	Being the #1 producer
Quota	A baseless objective	Objective to be met	The goal to be beat	The minimum bar to be crossed ASAP

How does a chef determine the quality of a particular dish? How much weight would he be likely to give to his own opinion or that of an underling? Probably not so much—as he would be unlikely to get useful, objective feedback. He is more likely to seek the opinion of his colleagues (or better yet, his superiors) and the general public who are the ultimate arbiters. And at what point is the master chef likely to say, "Well, gosh, this is good enough!" When? Never. He is always seeking to improve on his own work. He would seek out the work of others whom he considers better than himself and find ways to integrate some of their ideas into his menu. He is always trying to raise the bar. So it is with the passionate salesperson, the Maverick who is always seeking to improve his repertoire. He seeks the opinions of his colleagues and his superiors; he thrives on feedback and coaching because he knows that he cannot see his own swing. He actively seeks the opinions of others to keep himself honest and objective.

By way of extending the cooking analogy, we must add that chefs are not born. They are made. The man who does a mean burger for the family on the backyard grill for the Fourth of July does not generally rise to the quality of gourmet chef at a four-star restaurant. If he aspires to be a great chef, he must build his repertoire skill by skill, dish by dish, burger to steak to lamb chop!

The Matrix for the Lower Tier

If you are a B Player and do not aspire to be an A Player, do not give your manager this book! Managers will quickly learn the limits of the B Player and will be on the hunt for the Mavericks.

C Players are of course unlikely to be reading this book, but if you are, run and hide. The gig is up. Run, do not walk, to the nearest exit. If you are a C Player—and happy being a C Player—quit blaming everyone else and either get engaged or find something that excites you enough to get engaged. You will be found out sooner or later. You are but a place holder and will be replaced. Either get in the game or get out. You have it within your grasp to grow and develop. Do not stagnate. Do not give up. Get in the game. C Players are the first to be fired and the last to be hired. The C Player has really two options: decide that sales is what they want to do and to build or rebuild their skills or find another career path that better fits their skills and motivations.

Unlike selling skills, the Maverick method's strategies and processes are off-field activities—you can learn them in the privacy of your own home. You don't have to practice in front of live prospects with all the awkward stumbling about that usually entails. Indeed, when learning a new skill, sales often drop slightly for a short period while you get your sea legs. You will initially appear incongruent and stiff; you will be outside your comfort zone—but the payoff is fairly quick and well worth the trouble

By practicing the Maverick method before and after your calls, you will begin to get a better sense of the lay of the land: where the deal is, what you need to do next, and what might go wrong. Once you have incorporated the method into your sales style, you will have a framework to use, adding a sense of logic and reason versus the treasure hunt method.

How to Move from Being a C player to a B player

Reviewing the distinctions between the C and B player is the place to start, and it is clear that the major differences are in the attitudes. If the C Player has the base characteristic of intelligence, what is typically missing with the C Player is motivation to change his or her view of selling. The key attitude that needs to be changed is being emotionally attached to winning, which will have the C Player take responsibility for winning the deal. With the two pillars of selling success being intelligence and motivation, the seller will have the foundation to learn what is needed and the energy to make it happen. If the seller does not have the minimum intelligence, he or she will not be able to learn what is needed. The good news is that even with the minimum intelligence level and a large amount of motivation, the seller will be able to push himself to adapt to the environment. The most common cause of a seller being a C Player is just a lack of motivation to push himself to the next level.

How to Move from Being a B Player to an A Player

Moving from a B Player to an A Player requires much more than the transition of a C to a B. The characteristics must be there, but they are just not enough. The A Player has developed powerful skills that take years of practice and determination. The B Player who wants to grow and develop will need to first admit that his skill set needs to be developed. The trap that most B Players get stuck in is that they already feel that they are A Players. The obvious way to tell whether someone is an A Player or not is to see if they are able to produce the results consistently quarter after quarter. Often, a B Player with a great territory will get great results, and the B Player will grow to believe that it is his skill and not that he has been given the gift of a great territory. If the B Player can reflect on his abilities and ask for feedback, he will learn what his weak areas are and put a plan together to develop the skills to get to the A level.

With the majority of the salespeople falling into the B category, there are plenty of examples to examine what they do differently from their more successful peers. Managers like B Players because they do what they are told and are faithful workers. Within larger established companies, being a B Player is enough, and the B Player is seen as the desired team member. The challenge that the B Player will face is that if the company gets hit by a rough economy or an aggressive competitor, the B Player is outmatched. In the job market, the B Player will also find it hard to differentiate himself or herself from the herd of B Players.

How to Move from Being an A Player to a Maverick

Once the foundation of skills is integrated into the seller's personality, the difference between an A Player and a Maverick becomes their unique strategies. A Players will implement their own strategy, but like the great chefs of the world, each carves out his own niche. A Players will have developed the Maverick skill set of direction, momentum, and control, but they will then need to develop their own strategies that raise their talents to the Maverick level. Mavericks will be smart enough to know what their strengths are and strong enough to examine their weaknesses as well. Two of the general characteristics that separate A Players from Mavericks are the creative or independent thinking and radical approaches to winning deals. Mavericks do not limit themselves to corporate structure or the prospect's protocol. The Maverick redefines what is allowable and possible: they break through the limits and redefine what is possible. Some people simply do not have the creativity to define their own strategy, so they adopt the strategy of another Maverick.

The Matrix for Managers

From a manager's standpoint, the matrix is a useful tool for ranking his own team and for evaluating interviewees. If managers can properly rank their team members, they may begin to understand why they keep missing the forecast and losing deals. They may gain some insight into the personnel changes that would make them more competitive in the innovation selling environment.

Managers will gain great value by teaching and implementing the Maverick method; it provides a common language and, thus, facilitates communication. A process map, customized to your particular product, will help you know where to spend coaching time and will pinpoint where you actually are in relation to the potential closing of deals. It will also massively improve your forecasting accuracy.

The manager of C Players has been frustrated for quite a while, quite unable to prod them to move and make anything happen. C Players work only on the deals that are pulling them; they do not prospect or work on developing dormant accounts. The manager's question about C Players is simple: would we be better off having no one in the position? In most cases, they are better off, but barely. The managers will be looking to upgrade the position as soon as an opportunity presents itself. The mistake managers make is trying to change C Players; they do not want to change. They are burnt-out, or they just don't get it, or they're in the wrong job. If you are stuck with a C Player, try to move him to a position that will have the least negative impact possible.

Managers of B Players can quickly determine whether the B Players can grow into A Players by judging whether, first, they think they know it all. Managers know when they try to coach the B Player and just get smiles and nods. The B Player who feels that he knows it all and has done everything possible already does not understand what he is missing and is not taking responsibility. If B Players are confident enough to accept feedback and that have room for improvement, the manager can coach them with the distinctions that would take their selling to the next level.

Managers of A Players typically just count their blessing, but there is still considerable room to grow. When the A Player is competing in a new market with a new product, even the A Player will find it challenging and may even be competing against other A Players. Managers in very complex and highly competitive markets will need even A Players to rise to the Maverick level. The good news is that A Players want to be better, so management just needs to coach them and support them. By practicing the skills and developing their strategies, A Players can quickly rise to the Maverick level.

Maverick Skills	C Player	B Player	A Player	Maverick
Direction	Natural course	Follow the process	Push and pull	Set and lead
Momentum	Follow the customer	Driven by the quarterly deadlines	Has momentum with one or two players	Creates and maintains momentum
Control	The customer is in control	In control when the prospect wants something	Control is gained and lost as the deal becomes more complex	Controls the process from beginning to end

Stakeholder	C Player	B Player	A Player	Maverick
Customer	Vendor	Company's representative	Advocate	Team member
Manager	Dead weight	Solid contributor	Dependable	Rainmaker
Company	Burden	Company man	Rising star	Magician

The different views of the players reveal some very important distinctions and explain, again, why there are so few Mavericks. It becomes apparent that customers value the Maverick seller more than the company the Maverick works for. This is easily explained in that the customers see the value that the Maverick brings to their businesses and sense the difference that a Maverick seller makes. The company that the Maverick works for will have in fighting by less successful salespeople and their managers to explain the reasoning for the Maverick's success. The internal squabbling will be focused on saving face and diminishing the individual contribution of the Maverick, so the internal view will be muddied. The reader's natural reaction to the internal selling would be, if the Maverick is successful, a great salesperson, why doesn't he manage the internal representation of his work as well as the customer-facing work? Well, one the characteristics of Mavericks we have studied is that they shun the internal politics and thrive for the closing of deals. So the company does not know what to do with Mavericks. If they have the proper political support, unique positions will be created for them, and both Maverick and company will prosper.

Chapter 11

HOW TO IMPLEMENT THE MAVERICK METHOD

Because the Maverick method is an advanced selling method that focuses on the advanced techniques of the most successful salespeople, we will focus just on the skills and strategies that separate Mavericks from the crowd. Since the basic selling skills have been written about in hundreds of books and training programs, we see no real value in writing about them as part of this book. We want to focus on material that is new and not covered in any other book.

The assumption that we are making is that you will have the basic selling skills and have several years of selling experience. If you do not have the basic selling skills under your belt, it is more important to build those skills and review the laws and process, but without the basic skills, this method will not have the impact that you would expect. You will receive insights that you would not find anywhere else other then studying a Maverick in your organization.

The first step is to think like a Maverick. Leveraging the Maverick matrix, you will be able to understand the characteristics and attitudes that separate the Mavericks from the rest of the pack. The base characteristics are intelligence and motivation; we described these characteristics in the beginning of the book. Each of the other characteristics is built on intelligence and motivation. We will refer to the characteristics as the

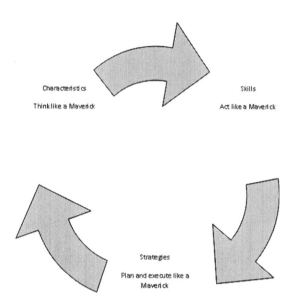

inner game of selling. There are literally hundreds of books on the inner game of selling, so we will not attempt to rewrite any of those great works here, but what we will do is make you aware that the characteristics are necessary building blocks.

Motivation is the why of selling: why I will work so hard, why I want to win, and why I cannot stand to lose. The why for each person is his or her own, and if the why is strong enough, then almost nothing else matters other than intelligence to know how to do it. We have all seen the highly motivated seller, the person who has two cell phones and meets with at least seven new people each day. These are the people that managers love to hire but wonder why they do not work out. They are analogous to an unguided missile: without a guidance system, the missile flies without a target and hits something valuable only by chance. Without properly applying intelligence, the salesperson will be lost and hides behind activity. Intelligence is needed for the complex sale because the process has not been fully developed, the prospects are sophisticated, and the competition is heavy.

Because there are hundreds of sources for building up one's motivation, let's focus on applying one's intellect to selling. The focus of the method is to understand the natural laws of selling, which are like rules to the game of selling, and the map to money, which is like the game board. The Maverick strategies will give you examples of how others have applied their unique skills to excel at winning deals. By developing the characteristics, developing the skills, and creating your own unique strategy, you will have the ability to separate yourself from the pack.

Proactive = Intelligent + Motivated

The characteristic of being proactive is a combination of applying intelligence and motivation. Being proactive is taking responsibility for the direction of the deal, knowing what to do next, and finding a way to make it happen. When you are proactive, you are taking control of the deal and becoming the owner of each step and action. By simply being proactive, a salesperson can rise to the A level. The method gives you the direction and insight into what the deal terrain looks like, so you will have the ability to know what to do next, what to do when something goes wrong, and what your competitor will do next.

Creative = Intelligent + Proactive

Being creative is applying your intellect and matching it with being proactive. The terrain will not stay static: the markets change, and competitors adapt quickly to new strategies. Creativity is needed to find new ways to build interest, to outsmart competitors, and to justify the investment in your product. Mavericks are very creative; they are independent thinkers and are even viewed as radical. An empowering question to ask is "What would the selling process look like if I ran the company?" This question will break down any of the limits that are in your way and allow you to come up with what is really needed to capture new clients and crush your competition. Developing your creativity may be difficult if you have been stuck in your limited view of what is possible. One exercise is simply to brainstorm for five minutes about how to move a deal forward or all the pain a prospect may be experiencing. Meeting with other salespeople or even other people in your company who will have a different vantage point will give you insights that you have not yet thought of.

Competitive = Proactive + Creative

To win a deal, you will need to be more competitive than the others who have alternatives for the money that funds your product. Competitiveness is the combination of being proactive and coupling it with creativity. Competitiveness becomes a more complex kind of motivation; it requires an emotional attachment to winning. Developing the characteristic of competitiveness has to do with an inner need to win and intolerance for losing. The trick is simple: You need to take it personally and emotionally, and you cannot let it go. You need to obsess on winning and refuse to lose.

The next step is to build the map to money for your particular product, but what if you have not sold the product yet? Well, you know the basic step of first call, technical win, and business win. There will be a wealth of knowledge among the sales team who has been successful in selling the product. The hard part in getting this information out of the salespeople is that you will need to ask very pointed questions about who was interested and why, what their role was, whether there was a competitor involved, and if so, what they did and when.

All this knowledge is most likely known but needs to be pulled out of the people who know it. Complex deals can take months, and the details of what worked can be overlooked with the "something magical happened," or the default reason becomes "because of the relationship that I built." Certainly, it could have been the relationship, but how was that relationship built, how did the salesperson get each key player to know that it was in his or her best interest to select the product, and what justified receiving money in exchange for it?

The next step is to identify who the typical players are:

1. Who is the person who will have the problem that your product will solve?
2. Who are the people that will need to determine whether the product will fit into their organization?
3. What are their titles, and which group do they work in?
4. Who is the technical leader?

Once you have your map to money drawn, you will be able to visualize the deal and apply the direction, momentum, and control.

The next step is to develop a strategy that will be used. The strategy can be built on one of the Maverick strategies or your own, but it needs to be thought out.

Before each call, consider the following:

1. What is the objective of the call?
2. What are the three things that they may ask for?
3. What are the top three things you can ask for in exchange for what they want?
4. What are the three things that can go wrong?
5. What are the three things that the competition has been doing?
6. What are the three things that you need to move the deal forward?
7. What are three ways of getting the next communication?

By thinking through the issues of the call, you will be prepared and know how to control, direct, and maintain momentum. It will take only fifteen minutes to outline the call, and after doing so for a month, it will become a natural part of your everyday process. The other benefit of thinking through the call in advance is that it gives you the ability to have a recovery strategy. If you have a well-thought-out response to the typical things that can go wrong, you will not be caught without a polished response.

During the call, attend to the following:

Bring everyone up to speed on how you arrived at this point. Ask what has changed since the last communication. Frame the objective of the meeting in a question and gain concurrence on the objective. To keep momentum and control over the deal, you will need to close for the next communication date. By simply putting your prep notes in your notebook in a way that you can read them and no one else can, you can refer to them during your meeting to make sure you cover every topic.

After the meeting, consider the following:

After each call, you should do your own postmortem to make sure you have a clear picture of the state of the deal. Document in your notes what actions you are responsible for. Review the natural laws of selling to give you a better sense of where you are on the map to money and what each player will do next.

What signals were given and how should I react to them?

Just remember the law of what isn't overtly positive is covertly negative.

Is your product seen as the favorite?

Were you able to get commitment to the next communication touch point? If not, why not, and do you really believe that their failure to commit to a date is not a negative signal?

The most common issue that people overlook is the fact that, in sales, there is an endless number of things to learn. The Mavericks take time to reflect on the maps that they build and each element. The Maverick determines the talents and skills that need development and identifies ways to develop those skills and talents. When you're developing a personal development plan, the key is to remember that skills take about a month to learn and integrate into one's personality, so it is important not to take on more than one new skill a month.

The method may seem like a lot of work, and at first, it may be, but after you have done several deals following the process, it will become natural. Soon you will be doing the method without having to review, and it will just be part of your personality. Without this method, it would take ten to twenty years for these skills to evolve and be integrated into your personality.

Interpersonal skills: Even though we are not covering these skills in this book, their need and importance is not diminished. As you develop your map and strategies, you will need to define the interpersonal selling skills that you will need at each stage of the map. The map will give you the terrain, but regardless of knowing where to go and how to go there, you will need strong interpersonal skills for selling.

> *I have no particular talent. I am merely inquisitive.*
> —Albert Einstein

What can go wrong with the method?

The most common struggle people have with the method is that they feel they are already doing it, and there is something outside of them that is in their way. The people who get the most value out of the method are those who spend the time, dig into the distinctions, and incorporate them into their own styles. The analogy that we use is to think of a time when you heard a comedian tell a joke that you thought was hilarious, but now, when you tell that same joke to your friends, they only smile. Did something happen to make that joke less funny? Maybe there is more to telling a joke than simply saying the words. If it was just saying the words, everyone could be a comedian.

Everyone likes the map concept, but few take the time to actually write the map up and think it through. Even if it only takes a couple of hours to write it up and review it, people feel that they can just do it in their heads, which they can, but imagine if you took just a few minutes a week and invested in your own map for selling your product. If you had a well-thought-out map before each call, you would know what is likely to happen and how to close for the natural next step. We purposely have not included a structured format for your map to money and leave it up to the individual to use the form that he or she is most comfortable with. Some people are comfortable with a spreadsheet and others with just using a notebook. Yes, it can even work if you have a great memory and visual skills: You can model your map in your mind, but this is rare. If you have a medium that can be edited and shared, your map can evolve and be refined. The salesperson who has a well-structured map has a great advantage over the salesperson.

You don't judge chefs on their recipes; you judge them on the dishes they produce.

The worst thing that sales management can do with the method is to mandate a standard map. The power of the method is that it is an individualistic approach to selling and not one of pushing people into a standard structure, regardless of how well-thought-out it is. Each map should be defined and owned by the individual sellers because they are the ones who will either win or lose. Sales management should encourage the testing of each map to push the salespeople to consider all the variables and instill a sense of competition as to who can develop the best way to handle each area of the sale. The map should be dissected and judged as a set of components and not judged as a whole. The sales team should be encouraged to share their perspectives on how best to handle each step. Managers will quickly be able to tell if their team is developing a map by simply asking during their forecast calls where they are in the deal and what they are going to do next. If the salesperson has a map, he or she will have a well-thought-out plan that follows a proven process.

Asking for help is the next biggest piece that is missing. Few people are brave enough to go to another salesperson and ask for feedback or compare approaches. We will spend years getting the same response. When we get feedback, we should dig into what is behind it and seek to understand how it is affecting our selling ability. The natural reaction to feedback is to defend our actions and to justify why we did not do anything wrong. Like with our cooking analogy, a sale is a lot like a complex dish: it can always be done better.

The Maverick method is intended to be a framework and an advanced reference for experienced sellers. By only reading the book, you will only receive insights into how great salespeople become great, but becoming a great seller requires a great deal of practice and refinement. If you use this book as a reference and integrate the method into your style, you will see a remarkable amount of growth.

Chapter 12

MANAGING MAVERICKS

The impact the Maverick seller can have on an organization can be amazing. Mavericks do not just do 10 percent better than A Players but typically one hundred to one thousand percent better. Mavericks single-handedly have created markets. So the need to hire the best possible salespeople is clear, and the need increases exponentially with the complexity of the sale. Too often, early market share is won not based on the merits of the product but the skill of the salespeople. Whichever company can attract the best salespeople will win the early adopters and gain enough of a lead as to marginalize the other competitors. As companies mature, the issues and requirements for the caliber of salespeople will change dramatically.

When interviewing and recruiting, the manager needs to look for the characteristics that make up the Maverick and look for evidence that the candidate has some of the skill set of direction, momentum, and control. The most common mistake during the hiring process is looking for the myth of the great salesperson. The myth of the hyperactive, outgoing personality is not the acid test of selling skills. The hiring manager needs to dig into the candidates' skill sets and what unique strategies they apply to selling. When interviewing, the hiring manager needs to be sensitive to the fact that Mavericks may not know how to articulate how they sell; like a great chef, they have a talent that they have not had to explain, so they are not good at explaining it. B and C Players are used to having to find new jobs, are much better at interviews, and know what hiring managers want.

Managers dream of hiring Mavericks and being able to go into each new fiscal quarter knowing that they will far exceed their quotas. Every manager knows that with every benefit, there is the other side that is less than positive. Mavericks, like most people, feel that the company's mission is the same: selling the product, beating the competition, and exceeding the customer's expectations. Companies that sell products are much like the companies that buy products; they are staffed with a diverse group of people, with each having his or her own agenda. The weakness of the Maverick is the belief that everyone in the company is behind him and completely aligned on the single-minded objective. The friction is caused by the Maverick in the field requesting help to capture the deal and those back at the home office wondering why they cannot just do it themselves.

The manager of Mavericks needs to learn that because the Mavericks know how to sell, the manager's job is to create the support systems for the Mavericks in the field. Few managers figure this out; they are more used to traveling and going out on sales calls with less experienced salespeople. The Maverick knows how to sell; what is missing is the support from the home office. The support Mavericks need may vary depending on what stage the company is in. At the early stages of the company's growth, it may be quick turnaround on product features or deep dive into future capabilities.

The situation that attracts Mavericks slowly disappears in the years after joining the company. The key attractions that excited the Mavericks, like the freedom to work independently and to have the whole organization with them, has changed dramatically.

"Revenue Solves All Problems"

The downside of hiring and even developing Mavericks is that they very quickly start doing their own thing, so it becomes a lot like herding cats. Organizations require at least a little bit of structure and consistency to have some level of control. Sales management of Mavericks can be tricky because management wants more than just outstanding revenue. Once a company moves past the early stages, the organization requires a greater amount of reporting, and the value of an individual superstar has less and less impact.

You would think that managing Maverick-quality salespeople would be a breeze because they would be more skilled at selling than their manager. Some of the side effects of independent thinkers who have their own unique way of doing things can be less than predictable to the executives within the organization. Mavericks, by nature, are not great with following the organization's rules and view a lot of the administrative tasks as a waste of time. These flaws can be overlooked when million-dollar deals are flowing in. Most of the Maverick's manager's time will be repairing the broken glass internally: people's feelings hurt by less than polite requests for support, expense reports that look like the shopping list of a bachelor party, and demanding e-mails that were sent to other members of the management team.

Jack was, in many ways, an idiot savant. When I first met Jack at the typical new salesperson training class, he appeared scatterbrained and even burnt out; he had a fantastic track record of success at his previous company. I know his new manager was not yet convinced that Jack was a keeper and thought that he might not even make it through the next quarter. At the evening group dinners, Jack would show up late and appeared disheveled, appearing as though this was the first time he has been in a restaurant. Several of the other new salespeople had seen this happen before when a bad hire took place, and it even seemed comical. Jack's behavior continued, and the concern expressed by several members of the executive team also increased, but it was too early to make a decision on Jack.

After the first quarter was over, Jack had closed the first deal that was over $500,000 in less than ninety days, and the sales team regrouped for our quarterly sales meeting. The other salespeople all had their justification for Jack's success and their lesser performance. Part of the justification for Jack's performance was that he had inherited the deal and that it was not completely his efforts that generated the $500,000 deal. Jack was feeling very happy with himself at the meeting. Each of the salespeople was required to prepare a presentation that reviewed the previous quarter and the outlook *for the next quarter. Jack's presentation was attended by the president of the company and several other executives, but Jack's prowess with PowerPoint, the presentation software, was less than proficient. Jack's presentation with his PowerPoint slides, which looked like a first grader had done them, was characterized by his manager as embarrassing. The president shook his head and walked out of the room.*

The second quarter was even better for Jack, with two deals that added up to over $900,000, about 30 percent of the start-up's revenue. Jack's success continued to give him a pass to behave any way he wanted, but his manager was getting frustrated with cleaning up after Jack and wanted to have Jack follow the company's selling activities, which included making a set number of sales calls per week and maintaining a sales plan for each forecasted deal. Jack ignored his manager and felt that he did not add any value to his selling efforts. Jack was correct in his assessment of his manager, but he was still his manager, and he needed to work with him.

The first year was a very successful year for Jack, with a two-million-dollar deal in the fourth quarter, knocking the ball out of the park. Even the president of the company became a Jack fan and cut Jack even more slack. Jack was a classic Maverick: he was completely independent and could not articulate what he did to close these amazing deals.

The next year, the company did what every company does. The CFO was very concerned that Jack was making more than anyone else in the company and that they could hire five salespeople for what they were paying Jack. The two-million-dollar deal had occurred the previous year, and there were new and higher expectations to meet, so the company cut Jack's territory and raised his quota. Jack did not feel valued for his contribution but liked the product and his prospects for the following year. The first quarter was a bust for Jack: not a single deal was closed, and he was once again looking more like the idiot and less like the savant. Jack's manager continued to push him into selling the way he wanted him to and adhering to the company's administrative standards. The friction built to the point where Jack would not return his manager's calls. Jack wanted to report to the president of the company and work on the large deals that he liked to work on.

After the second quarter with less than $50,000 of revenue, Jack's manager had the case built to have Jack fired. The memory of the first year was not enough to keep Jack afloat. Of course, the three people who took over Jack's territory did less than a quarter of the revenue that Jack had done, but they did keep their sales administration plans in order. Jack was not missed, but his revenue certainly was.

Mavericks are management challenges in many ways, but the alternative is the failure of the company to make its objectives and losing it market segment. In the early stages of a company, each hire is critical to the company's success, and each mistake can be catastrophic. Small early stage companies are wasting their time and money hiring anyone who is not at least an A Player. Each deal and every new customer you capture is one that your competitor is not getting, and if it is a kingpin, it can be the difference between being the leader in the market segment and being just a distant runner-up.

As the organization grows, the management team focuses on expansions and requires layers of management; thus, past relationships and priorities change dramatically. The financial upside has also been played out, with stock options having been fully vested and the opportunity to exceed the quota objectives being more limited. The structure and reporting of a larger organization can become a frustration for the Maverick who has been used to moving unencumbered from these oversights.

With the need for a larger sales organization, it is no longer possible to continue to fill each role with Mavericks for several reasons. First, the sales process has become simpler: The product has been accepted as the market leader, so competing is no longer as difficult. The speed with which the salespeople need to be hired does not allow for the long search time and high compensation. The B Players that would have been deadly at the early stages are now the target candidates for the rapid expansion stage.

It is rare that the management team will create unique positions for the Mavericks who wish to keep the same level of reward and independence that they have experienced during the rapid growth phases. Slowly but consistently, both the company and the Maverick lose interest in each other because they continue to be less and less of a match.

If the Mavericks wish to stay, they can still add outstanding value in several areas that will still justify their above-normal compensations. What we have seen work in the past is to work on global accounts or new target markets that bring significant growth. Other roles can be as a coach that would help bring the new sales teams up to speed and as a mentor.

There are some key reason for making sure the Mavericks do not leave too early. First, the product is ready for prime time and does not require a lot of customization or integration within the customer base. Second, if the sales process has not been codified, meaning that each deal is different than the previous, and remains highly complex, it will take too long to hire and train new salespeople, thus, making the value of existing people much higher. If several of the Mavericks leave too early, it opens a door for a competitor, who can pounce on the window of opportunity that will be created with the time delay of having to replace them, and it may create creditability issue with existing customers. Another coming issue that can happen with neglecting the Maverick is that a competitor will be more than willing to exceed its compensation package in order to bring someone who knows how to win and teach the rest of the team.

Often, the successful company will be in the process of either being sold or going public; either brings along with it a great deal of change and turmoil. The acquisition of the company will bring many issues, depending on the acquiring company's objectives and perception of the need to retain the sales force.

With an IPO comes a new level of oversight and reporting that raises the level of visibility and transparency of the company. The side effects of the new changes transcend all the teams within the organization. Within the sales organization, the individual compensation can become a concern if a few people's income is disproportionately higher than the norm. Quickly, the logic will shift from a "whatever it takes" attitude to one of "if we pay one person 500,000, why can't we get five people and pay them 100,000?" The focus turns to profitability versus growth.

The need for Maverick-level salespeople does not go away regardless of the size of the company, but as the company gets larger and larger, the tolerance for unique or special treatment becomes increasingly lower. Regardless of market share, there is always someone who is out there trying to change the rules and redefine the marketplace. The approach that larger companies can take is to take the "skunk works" approach.

At one of the largest technology companies, they created a start-up within their organization. Everything was separated, but the administration functions. This move allowed different rules to apply to each of the groups so that they would be able to work in the way they needed to compete in their marketplace. They could hire their own level of salespeople, with their own compensation plans and stock options. If the separate group had been required to use the existing sales organization, it would surely have failed because the new product required a new set of skills. This strategy has worked before but requires strong leadership that can keep the larger parent corporation from losing faith.

Skunk works

In the 1940s, Lockheed solved the problem of keeping its Maverick engineers motivated and productive by separating them into a small group, which they called Skunk Works. They had control over their own staff, style, and budget. This radical approach was actually not just kept separate but also secret. Kelly Johnson, the leader of the group of the Skunk Works team, was the strong leader who was able to select his team and had the freedom to execute his vision. Johnson was able to deliver the advanced aircraft and the supporting technology in a fraction of the time and within a smaller budget.

Few companies can execute the skunk works strategies successfully, and we rarely have seen it done well. The other common approach is that a larger company will acquire a smaller company with a successful product. The thinking is that, with the larger sales force and customer population, the new product can just be plugged in. This approach often fails because the acquired product has its own market and competitors, and to have an untrained or junior salesperson compete for a customer against someone who sells only this product does not work. The acquiring sales management team most likely does not have experience managing Mavericks. The larger companies are largely populated with B and C Players who can skate by just selling more and more to the install base.

Managers who are unable to create a challenging and interesting opportunity for the Mavericks on their team will find letters of resignations on their desks. The only thing worse than the resignations is having the Mavericks growing more and more disgruntled. The managers need to find new situations for the Mavericks to use their talents, which can include teaching less-experienced salespeople or targeting new market segments.

There will be cases in which the Maverick becomes such a mismatch for the organization as to no longer have a place within it. Such a situation is unfortunate but must be dealt with quickly and fairly. Mavericks will have no problem finding a new opportunity but may need the push to make it happen before the situation sours further. The most important problem to prevent is having the Maverick go to a competitor where he or she can teach the skills to an army of salespeople hungry for market share. It is the manager's responsibility to give the Maverick the support in finding a new noncompetitive opportunity and to support the effort with recommendations. When done well, the exit will be graceful without anyone being bitter or resentful.

Index